Collins

Tree of Life 3

A Course on Environmental Studies

Dinu Raheja
Lipika Ghosh

Student + Teacher			Teacher-only	
a animations	**ia** activities	**g** games	**lp** lesson plans	**tn** teacher's notes
ilt instructor-led tutorials	**w** worksheets	**v** videos	**w** worksheets	**ak** answer keys
	audio			

Preface

Tree of Life Updated Edition is an engaging and innovative course on Environmental Studies for classes 1 to 5. It adopts a multidisciplinary approach to ensure holistic learning for young learners. This series of five books adheres to the National Education Policy, 2020. An interactive and learner-centric course, *Tree of Life* has planned pedagogical elements that help learners connect social, cultural and scientific concepts with real-life situations. Promoting experiential learning, learners are encouraged to explore their immediate world and foster environmental awareness. The well-graded content has been created keeping in mind several goals—easy readability, accuracy and creativity. At the same time it empowers learners towards higher levels of academic scholarship.

The concepts in the series are presented simply, supplemented by colourful pictures and illustrations. Varied key features in the series hone learning skills.

- Multidisciplinary and a holistic education—**Exploration Station, Cross connect**
- Life skills and making ethical decisions—**Learn the ropes**
- Creativity, art integration, creating joyful classrooms—**Put your heads together**
- Organic living—**Poster, United Nations Sustainability Development Goals**
- A rootedness and pride in India—**Our Heritage**
- Inquiry-based, discovery-based, discussion-based, and analysis-based learning—**Get the ball rolling, Clued in, Give it a shot**
- Application and problem-solving—**Think through, Covid-19 Safety**
- Exploratory activities and experiential learning—**Why it Works**
- Moving towards real understanding and towards learning how to learn—**Wrap up**
- Assessment—**Brush up**

It is our endeavour to help the learners develop a responsible attitude towards the preservation of their environment.

- Authors

About the authors

Dinu Raheja, an innovative educationist and administrator, recipient of the International Teacher's Award, has over 15 years of teaching experience in Indian and international schools. Formerly, Middle School Incharge, Sanskriti School, New Delhi, she is currently Program Director with The Global Education & Leadership Foundation (tGELF). Dinu also facilitates teacher leadership development workshops.

Lipika Ghosh has over 25 years of teaching experience at St. Xavier's School Hazaribagh, Sardar Patel Vidyalaya, New Delhi and Sanskriti School, New Delhi. She has used innovative teaching methodology to make science a process of discovery interspersed with anecdotes for learners. Lipika has taught analytical skills and inculcated awareness of social issues amongst learners through science.

Key Features

Tree of Life Updated Edition is an engaging and innovative course on Environmental Studies for classes 1 to 5. The series adheres to the National Education Policy, 2020 and adopts a multidisciplinary approach to enable holistic learning.

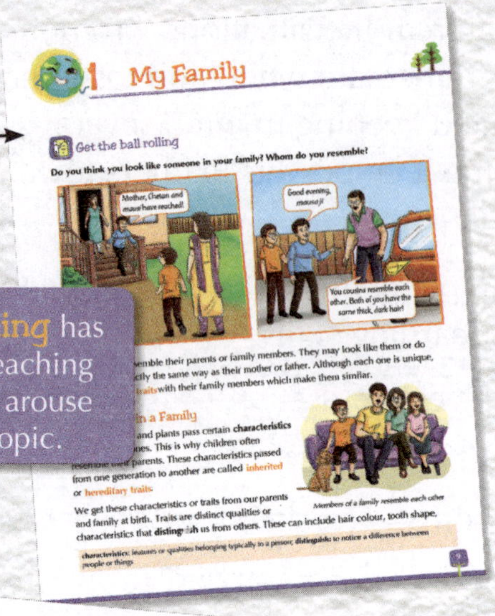

Get the ball rolling has compelling pre-teaching warm-up tasks to arouse interest in the topic.

Give it a shot promotes experiential learning through application-based activities.

Think through provides referencing tasks to develop critical thinking skills of the learners.

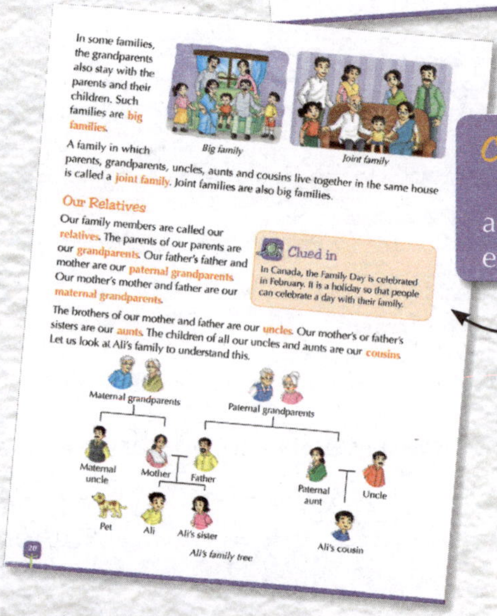

Clued in provides interesting additional facts for extended learning.

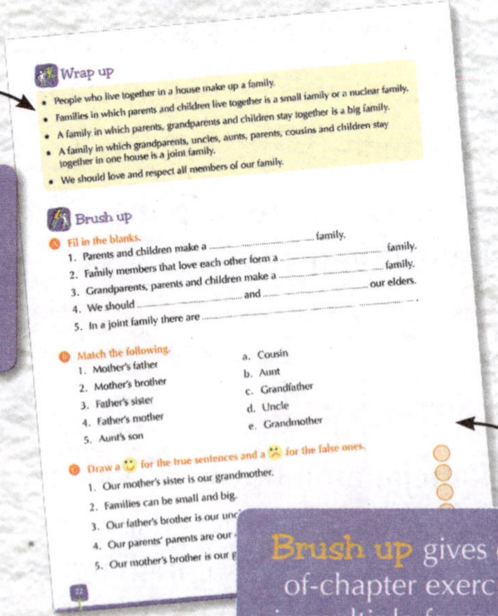

Wrap up provides a ready reckoner to reinforce the concepts taught for comprehensive learning.

Brush up gives end-of-chapter exercises in multiple formats to facilitate assessment.

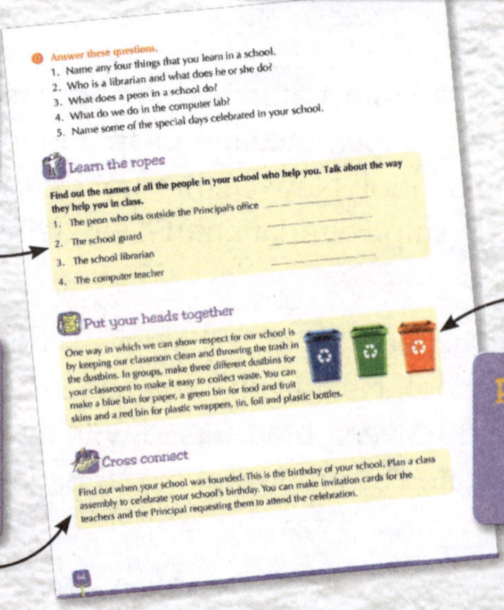

Learn the ropes provides activities for application of 21st century life skills.

Put your heads together provides group projects to strengthen teamwork and cooperative learning.

Cross connect tasks promote cross-disciplinary and integrated learning.

Why It Works provides experiments to promote scientific temper and hone observation skills of learners.

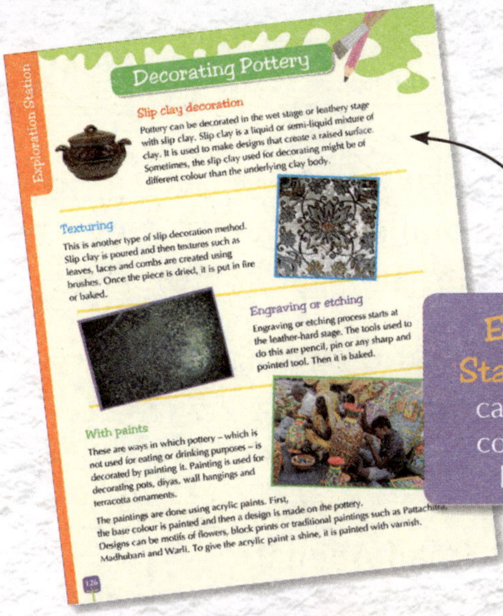

Exploration Station provides case studies for comprehensive knowledge.

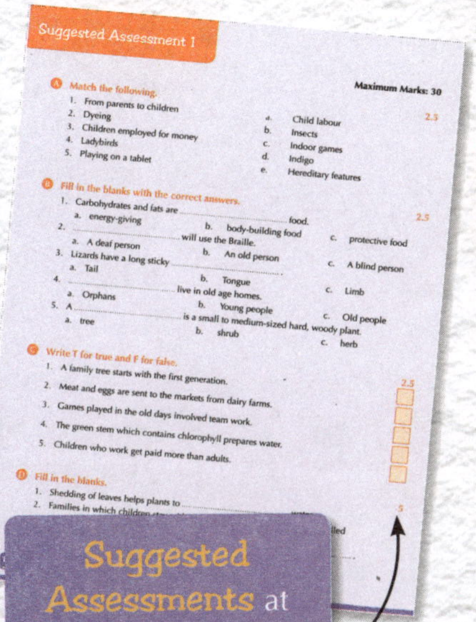

Suggested Assessments at the end of the book facilitate cumulative assessment.

Covid-19 Safety teaches students to stay safe and healthy.

Our Heritage provides snippets of information about the heritage of India and encourages learners to preserve it.

United Nations Sustainability Development Goals featured in specific sections to achieve a just and equitable world for all.

Poster on 5Rs sensitizes learners towards their surroundings and creates awareness about sustainability of the environment.

Contents

1 My Family and I

Get the ball rolling

Look at these pictures. Do some of these family members resemble each other? Whom do you resemble in your family? Do you look like your mother or father?

A **family** is a group of people who live together. Parents, brothers, sisters, grandparents, uncles, aunts and cousins are called **family members**. Families give us love and protection. We feel safe with our family members because they look after us.

Types of Families

Families are of three types—**nuclear families**, **joint families** and **single-parent families**. Families in which the mother, father and children live together are called **nuclear families**. Nuclear families are small. Children from these families visit their grandparents, uncles and aunts during holidays or over the weekends.

Nuclear family

Families in which grandparents live with mother, father and children are **big families**.

Families in which grandparents, uncles, aunts, parents, cousins and children live together are called **joint families**. Joint families are bigger than nuclear families. Families in which children stay with either mother or father are called **single-parent families**.

> **Clued in**
>
> The International Day of Families is celebrated every year on 15 May to celebrate the importance of families.

Big family

Joint family

Single-parent family

Family Relations

Family members who are related to each other are called **relatives**. Parents of our father and mother are our **grandparents**. Our father's parents are our **paternal grandparents**. Our mother's parents are our **maternal grandparents**. We are the **grandchildren** of our grandparents. We call our grandparents by special names such as *nana, nani, dada* and *dadi*. Are there any other names by which you call your grandparents?

> **Think through**
>
> How do you keep in touch with your relatives?

Similarly, our mother's brother is our **maternal uncle**. Our mother's sister is our **maternal aunt**. We call them *mama* and *mausi*. Our father's brother is our **paternal uncle**. Our father's sister is our **paternal aunt**. We call them *chacha* and *bua*. What do you call your maternal and paternal aunts and uncles? The children of our aunts and uncles are our **cousins**.

Family Generations

Family members who are born and grow old in the same period are said to belong to the same **generation**. Our grandparents belong to the **first generation**. Their children are our parents, uncles and aunts. They form the **second generation** of the family. We, along with our brothers, sisters and cousins belong to the **third generation**. The parents of our grandparents are our **great-grandparents**. They are called our **ancestors**.

The many generations of a family can be **recorded** with the help of a **family tree**. A family tree shows the people of a family for many generations and their relationship with each other. A family tree always begins with grandparents or great-grandparents.

recorded: to set down in writing

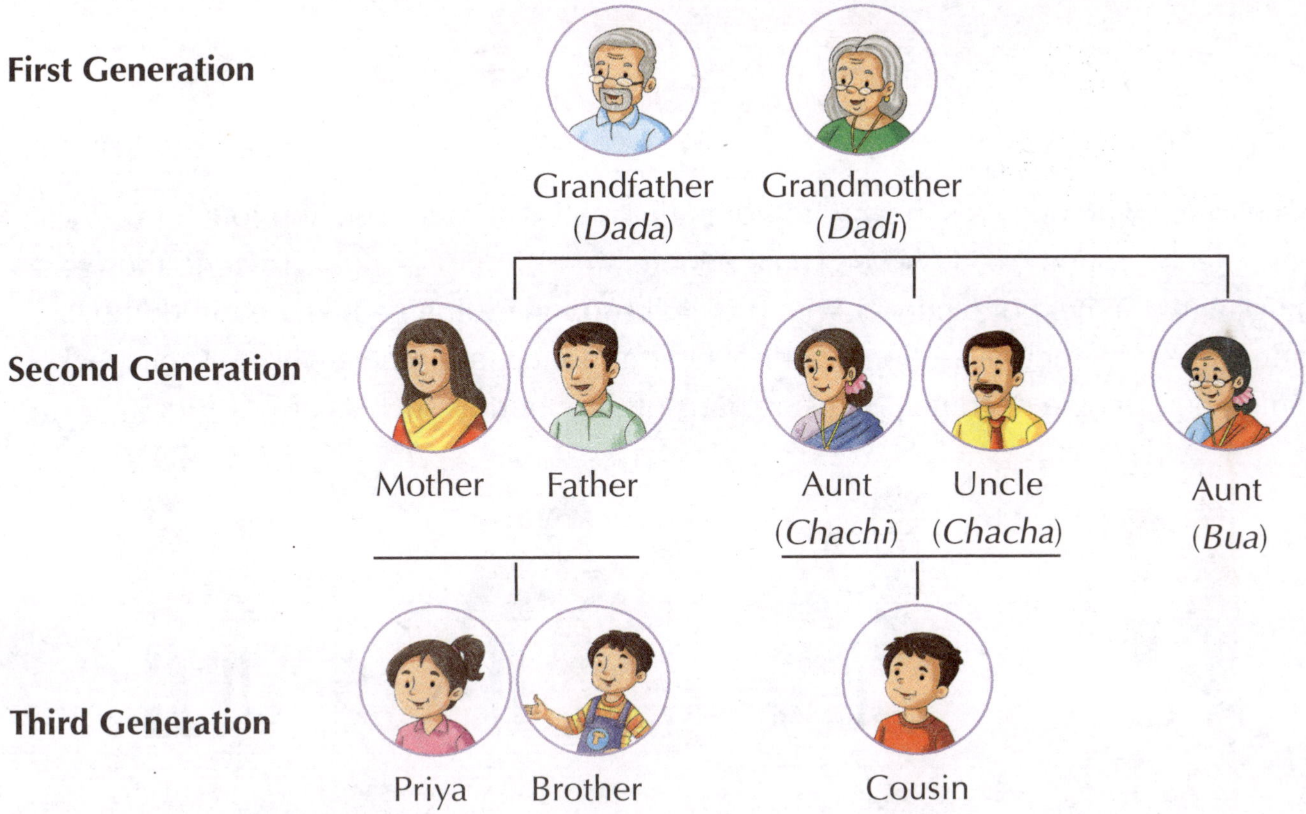

Three generations of Priya's family

Family Resemblances

Family members resemble each other

People often tell us that we look like our father and mother. This is because family members look a lot like each other and might have similar **appearances**. This is called **family resemblance**.

Children often have features like that of their parents. A child might have eyes, nose or hair colour similar to that of his or her parent. Such features that are passed down to children from their parents are called **hereditary features**.

Twins

Brothers and sisters also resemble each other. Two children who are born at the same time to the same mother are called **twins**. Twins who look exactly like each other are called **identical twins**. However, some twins do not look exactly like each other. They are called **fraternal twins**.

Family members also resemble each other in their habits. A **habit** is a behaviour that is often repeated. Some family influences are also passed down to the children from parents or grandparents. Often, we take part in the same activities that our grandparents or great-grandparents took part in. Such activities can include sport, art and dance, amongst many others. This is because we feel **inspired** by our family members.

appearances: the way a person looks; **inspired**: to give a person an idea about something

Be Caring

We can see with our eyes, hear with our ears, smell with our nose and touch to feel objects around us. However, some people are **differently-abled**. They do these things with the help of others or with medical support. Some people are blind; they cannot see with their eyes. Some cannot hear and there are others who cannot speak. Sometimes, people need help in using parts of their bodies such as arms or legs.

All of us need help to do many things. Differently-abled people sometimes need more help than we do and we should be sensitive to their needs. There are many ways in which we can help them.

- We should never make fun or laugh at differently-abled people.
- Everyone needs love and care, just like the differently-abled. Always show respect towards other people despite their differences.
- Pay attention to the needs of others.
- Always offer to help friends or classmates if they find difficulty in doing something on their own. Remember to ask them just once; they might not need as much help as you think they do.

In 1824, Louis Braille invented the Braille Script, which made it possible for the blind to read and write. Braille is a series of raised dots that can be felt with the fingers as the person moves his or her hand over the page. The letters are identified by touching the raised dots.

Orphans are children who have lost their parents. Some of these children have relatives to care for them. However, some of them live on their own. Some of them might also live in special homes called **orphanages** where they get shelter, clothes, safety and food. We should help these children by **donating** food, clothes, study material and books to orphanages.

When we are young, we are strong and **energetic**. As we grow older, our energy levels go down. Therefore, old people need help and care. Some old people cannot live with their families. They live in **old age homes** where they are taken care of.

There are different ways in which we can care for the elderly:

- We should help old people do activities that might be difficult for them. For example, we can help our grandparents climb the stairs.
- We should spend time with them because many old people don't go out of their homes very often.
- We should help them take their medicines on time.
- We should not talk loudly or play loud music when they are resting.
- We should offer them our seats in a bus or in a metro.

donating: giving money or goods for a good cause; **energetic**: full of energy

Together as a Family

We learn **values** such as honesty, kindness, care and responsibility from our families. We learn how to care for one another and how to share our things with our brothers and sisters. The elders in the family teach us how to respect others. We also learn to be helpful and thoughtful towards other people and their needs.

We learn to be helpful from our family

The **traditions** and **customs** followed by our families are also passed on to us. Each family has their own practices, for instance, no mobile phones at the dinner table, washing up before dinner, leaving the shoes on the shoe rack near the door and not bringing shoes inside the house. Big or small—members of a family help each other with the household work as well. Children too help in the household work by setting the table for dinner, putting their toys and books back in their places, keeping their rooms tidy and watering plants in the summer months.

A family is a happy family when all members of the family spend time with each other, **communicate** with each other, have dinner together and celebrate all festivals together.

Give it a shot

Look at this family tree and fill in the relationship gaps. Also, write what you call these relations in your family. You may add more boxes if required.

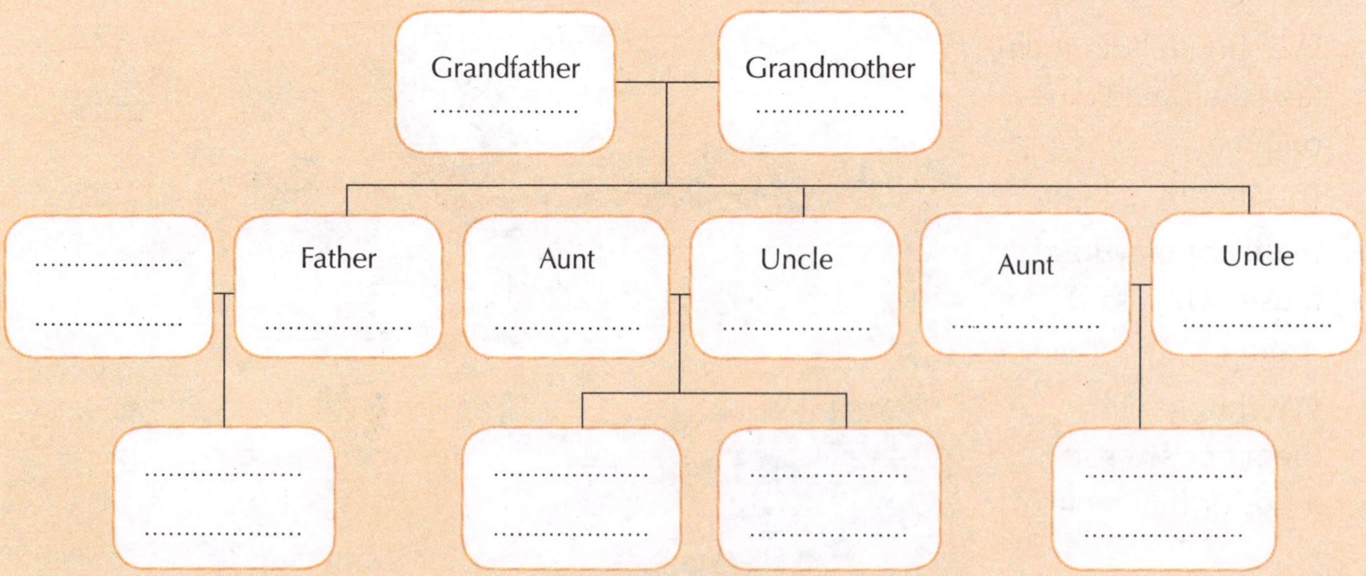

values: beliefs that are important in life; **traditions**: a belief that has existed for a long time; **customs:** practices that are common to a particular place or class; **communicate:** to talk, converse or convey information and ideas

Wrap up

* The different types of families are nuclear family, big family, joint family, and single-parent family.
* In a family, members are related to each other. They are called relatives.
* A family tree shows the different generations of a family and how they are related.
* Resemblance to a family member is hereditary as it is passed down from one generation to another.
* We learn values, family customs and traditions from our families.

Brush up

A Answer in one word.

1. My father's father is my ....
2. My mother's brother is my ....
3. My father's daughter is my ....
4. My uncle's son is my ....
5. My father's sister is my ....

B Fill in the blanks.

1. A .... family has parents and children living together.
2. A big family has ...., ... and ....
3. People who are related to each other in a family are known as ....
4. A family tree always starts with the .... They form the first .... in the family.
5. Physical features that are passed down from one generation to another are called .... features.

C Write T for true or F for false.

1. Families teach us to fight with others. ☐
2. Festivals give us an occasion to meet our relatives who do not live with us. ☐
3. We learn values and customs from our families. ☐

4. A family tree starts with the third generation.

5. A family with uncles, aunts and cousins living in the same house is a nuclear family.

D Answer these questions.

1. How is a joint family different from a big family?
2. What is a single-parent family?
3. What are the similarities between the different types of families?
4. What do you understand by family resemblance?
5. What are some of the values and habits you have learnt from your family?

Learn the ropes

What are some of the customs and traditions followed in your family? From your grandparents, find out about two such customs or traditions and why they are followed.

Put your heads together

People who are deaf and mute use a sign language and express themselves using their fingers. In groups, make a chart on the signs used to show feelings such as thirsty, excited, sick, hungry, sad and tired.

Cross connect

Make birthday cards for your grandfather and your grandmother and be the first to wish them on their birthdays.

2 Plants Around Us

Get the ball rolling

How many kinds of plants do you see in this picture? What differences do you notice?

Humans depend on plants directly or indirectly for many things. Most of what we have comes from plants. Food, shelter, clothes, medicines, furniture, paper and rubber, amongst many other things, all come from plants.

Types of Plants

We see different kinds of plants around us. They are different in shape, size and colour. Some are big and some are small; some are found on land and some in water.

Plants are of different shapes and sizes

Trees are plants that are tall, big and strong. They have thick, strong and woody stems called **trunks**. Trees have a long life and some even live for a thousand years. The trunk of a tree is covered with a **protective** layer called **bark**. Some trees **shed** most or all of their leaves once

protective: a thing that protects something; **shed**: to drop something in a natural way a year, whereas others remain green throughout the year. Some common trees are mango, banyan, neem, coconut, gulmohar and peepal.

Neem

Çoconut

Banyan

Gulmohar

A **shrub** or a **bush** is a small to medium-sized hard, woody plant. Such plants live for a few years. Some examples are hibiscus, lilac, bougainvillea, rose and lime.

Rose bush

Bougainvillea

Herbs are small and have soft green stems. They live only for one season. Grass is a herb. Some commonly grown herbs are mint, coriander and spinach.

Coriander

Mint

Some plants have weak stems that need support to grow. Such plants grow with the help of a stick, a wall or another tree growing adjacent to it. These plants are called **climbers**. Some examples are grapevines, money plant, morning glory and bean plants.

Creepers are plants with weak, soft stems that grow along the ground. Muskmelon, watermelon, gourd and pumpkin are common examples.

Grapevine

Plants in Different Climates

Plants need **air**, **water**, **sunlight** and **soil** to grow. The climate of a place decides the type of soil, water availability and the type of plant that grows in a place. Plants grow in the plains, mountains, forests, deserts and in very cold regions. Plants are found under water as well. The Ashoka tree, cotton, neem, wheat and rice grow in the plains. Coconut palms grow in places where it rains

Rice grows in plains

often and where there is plenty of sunlight throughout the year. **Rainforests** grow in places that are hot and **humid**. In places where it is neither too hot nor too cold, trees such as apple and mango grow in **orchards** or **groves**. Dry and thick grasses grow in hot and dry places. Date palms and cacti survive very well in desert conditions. Pine, fir and birch grow well on mountains that are covered by a thick layer of snow in winter. In the **Arctic region**, plants grow close to the ground. Some plants like duckweed, lotus, lily and water hyacinth are found in water. These plants are known as **aquatic plants**. They die when they are taken out of water.

Think through

How do plants reduce pollution in our surroundings?

Cacti

Apple tree

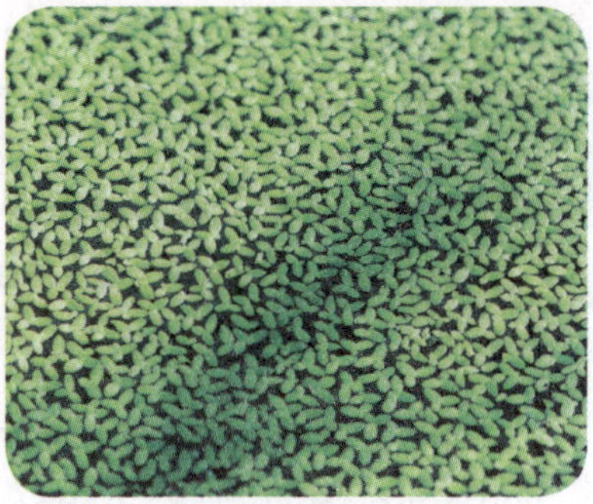

Duckweed

Clued in

The tallest tree ever was an Australian eucalyptus. In 1872, it was measured at 435 feet.

Today, we find many fruits and vegetables that were not available before. Some of these fruits are kiwis from New Zealand, apples from Washington and raspberries from Europe. Some of these vegetables found in the market are broccoli, asparagus and Chinese cabbage. They are not locally grown in places where we live.

Exotic plants are those plants which are brought from other countries and are growing well in our country. For example, vanilla was brought from Mexico, litchi has come from China and kinnow from California.

Litchi

Vanilla

Give it a shot

Find out the names of five fruits which were not available and not eaten by people living in your grandparent's time but are available in the market now.

rainforest: a forest in a hot area that receives a lot of rain; **humid**: air containing high amount of water vapour; **orchard**: an area of land in which fruit trees are grown; **grove**: a group of trees that are close together; **Arctic region**: the region around the North Pole

Plants Are Our Friends

Plants are very useful to us.

- Plants give us oxygen, food, flowers, shade and shelter. They keep the air fresh and clean by taking in carbon dioxide and giving out oxygen, which is important for the survival of human beings and animals.
- We get different kinds of food such as fruits, vegetables, nuts, spices, sugar, tea, coffee, oil, wheat and rice from plants.
- Plants provide us various **fibres** such as cotton and jute. These fibres are yarns which are woven to make cloth. Coconut and jute fibres are used to make clothes and bags. Coconut provides us coir, which is a special fibre. Coir is used to make mats, rugs and mattresses.
- Trees such as teak, sheesham and mahogany provide us wood for making furniture.
- Trees provide us **medicines**. Tulsi, neem, ginger, eucalyptus and clove are medicinal plants.
- Trees provide many other things like rubber, paint, oil, cream, soap, toothpaste, perfume and varnish. Paper is produced from the bamboo plant. Dyes are produced from beetroot, indigo and henna (mehndi).

Fruits and vegetables

Coir mat

Teak plantation

Eucalyptus oil

Medicinal plants

Jute

Wrap up

- Plants are of different types. Some plants are found on land and some in water.
- Plants can be classified into trees, herbs, shrubs, climbers and creepers.
- Plants grow according to the climate and the soil. They also grow in water.
- Different plants need different amounts of water to grow.
- Plants are useful to us in many ways.
- Plants which are brought from other countries and are growing well in our country are known as exotic plants.

Brush up

A Fill in the blanks.

1. Plants keep the air fresh and clean by taking in .... and giving out ....
2. .... and .... are used to make clothes and bags.
3. Plants need .... , ... and sunlight to grow.
4. .... and .... are examples of exotic plants.
5. .... and .... are examples of climbers.

B Match the following.

1. Medicines	a. Bamboo
2. Furniture	b. Indigo
3. Paper	c. Tulsi
4. Coir	d. Mahogany
5. Dye	e. Coconut

C Write T for true or F for false.

1. Cacti grow in places that receive good rainfall. ☐
2. Rainforests grow in places that are hot and humid. ☐

3. Some exotic plants are vanilla and litchi.

4. Herbs are hard, woody plants.

5. Plants keep the air fresh by taking in carbon dioxide.

D **Answer these questions.**

1. What is a tree? Give some examples.
2. How is a herb different from a shrub?
3. How is a climber different from a creeper?
4. Write four important uses of plants.
5. Name two plants that grow in
   a. mountains b. deserts c. water d. plains

Learn the ropes

Choose any one of these plants—trees, shrubs, herbs, climbers and creepers. In an album or a notebook, paste pictures of the types of plants, write their names where they grow and list their important characteristics.

Put your heads together

In groups, make a list of fruits and vegetables that are grown now but were not available earlier. Make a table with four columns: name, taste, country of origin and in the fourth column, paste the pictures of the fruits and vegetables.

Cross connect

1. Take three saplings and keep each sapling under the following conditions:

   Sapling 1: Keep it closed in a shoe box and water it regularly.

   Sapling 2: Keep it in an open area but do not water it.

   Sapling 3: Keep it in an open area and water it regularly.

   Observe them for three weeks. What do you notice?

2. Write a poem on 'Plants and its Uses'.

3. Draw a cartoon strip in which plant is the superhero.

3 Leaves Around Us

Get the ball rolling

When do leaves fall? Are all leaves green in colour? Have you seen leaves of colours other than green? What are the uses of leaves?

Leaves are one of the most important parts of a plant. They are known as **food factories** because they make food for the plant. The leaves of different plants vary widely in size, shape and colour. A **leaf** is a flat structure growing from the stem or branch of a plant. Its main function is to make food for the plant by a process known as **photosynthesis**.

Parts of a Leaf

The broad part of a leaf is called a **leaf blade**. The **main vein** and **side veins** carry food and water in a leaf. They also support the blade.

Leaves have **stomata** on their underside. Stomata are small pores that help the plants breathe. These stomata take in carbon dioxide and give out oxygen. The **leaf stalk** or **petiole** is the part that attaches the leaf to the stem.

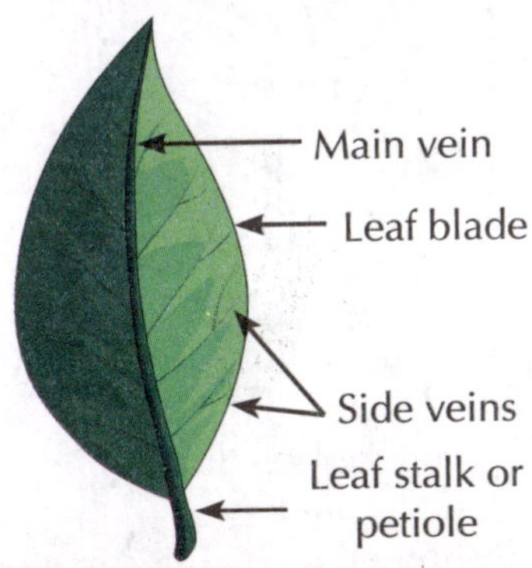

Parts of a leaf

stomata: one of the many pores on a leaf or stem of a plant through which gases are able to pass in and out

Different Kinds of Leaves

Leaves of different plants differ in colour, shape, size, smell and touch.

Colour: Most leaves are green due to the presence of a **pigment** called **chlorophyll**, which helps plants make food using water, air and sunlight. The leaves of some plants like croton, caladium and coleus are red, orange, yellow and purple in colour.

Caladium leaf

Coleus leaves

Croton leaf

Size and shape: Some leaves are big like papaya and lotus leaves and some are small like neem and tamarind leaves. Banana leaves are broad and long, lotus and water lily leaves are big and round, peepal leaves are heart-shaped and the leaves of the guava tree are **oval**. There are some leaves which are hand-shaped, some are **spear**-shaped and some are needle-shaped.

Water lily leaf

Peepal leaf

Special leaves: In desert plants like cactus, leaves are reduced to spines to **conserve** water. The green stem which contains chlorophyll prepares food. The aloe vera plant also stores water in its leaves, hence they are thick.

Aloe vera

Cactus with spines

Smell and texture: Some leaves such as coriander, mint, curry leaves and tulsi have a **distinct** smell. This helps us to identify them. When we touch leaves, they feel different for different plants. Some leaves are thin and soft, some are rough and some are thick and smooth. The leaves of basil and neem are soft, those of sunflower and rose plant have a rough **texture** and those of the rubber plant are **leathery**.

Rubber tree leaves

Neem leaves

Rose leaves

Sunflower leaves

pigment: a colouring matter in plants and animals; **chlorophyll**: the green substance in plants that allows them to use the energy from the Sun; **spear**: a weapon with a pointed tip; **conserve**: save; **distinct**: different or separate from something else; **texture**: the way a thing feels when we touch it; **leathery**: thick and smooth

Give it a shot

Collect some fallen leaves. Choose five leaves among those and draw them on a sheet of paper. Look at the veins, shape and texture of each and note them down.

Types of leaves

Leaves can be simple or compound. A **simple leaf** has a single leaf blade. A **compound leaf** has several leaflets.

Simple leaf

Compound leaf

Uses of Leaves

Apart from making food for the plant, leaves have many other uses.

- The oxygen that we breathe is released by the leaves during the process of photosynthesis.
- We eat leaves such as spinach, cabbage, fenugreek (*methi*) and betel.
- We use leaves of some herbs such as thyme, coriander and mint for flavour and fragrance.
- Leaves like bay leaf and dried fenugreek (*kasuri methi*) are used as spices.
- The leaves of plants such as neem and tulsi are used as medicines.
- The dried leaves of henna and indigo are used for dyeing hair and clothes.
- In east and south India, people sometimes serve food on banana leaves during festivals and special occasions.
- In some places, the leaves of certain plants like banyan, sal, palash or tesu are used as disposable plates called *pattal* and *dona*.
- The leaves of palm, coconut and date palm are used to make roofs.
- The powdered leaves of henna are used for making designs on palm and feet, known as mehndi.
- In tea, we use dried leaves of the tea plant.

Think through

Tithi found a branch of small leaves. How will she know if it is a simple leaf or a compound leaf?

Thyme

Bay leaf

Food served on banana leaf

Henna leaves and powder

Dry tea leaves

- Leaves of the Ashoka tree and mango tree are used for decoration.
- Leaf designs are used in block printing on cloth and paper. They are also used on potteries and walls of houses.

Mango leaves decoration

Shedding of Leaves

Once a year, many plants shed their leaves. These leaves are dry and lose their chlorophyll. Thus, there is a change in colour and texture. Some shed leaves throughout the year. Some shed all their leaves once a year. Sometimes leaves fall when the plants do not get enough water as it helps the plants conserve water.

Chinar leaf in autumn

Aspen trees change colour in autumn

Every autumn, as the days get shorter, trees across the world produce spectacular display of colours of leaves. Examples are chinar, maple and aspen.

Clued in

Oak leaves turn red, brown poplars turn golden-yellow, sugar maples turn orange-red, black maples turn a glowing yellow and red maple turn scarlet in autumn.

Compost

Fallen leaves are used to make **compost**, which is used as **fertilizer** and restores the lost nutrients of the soil. The leaves are collected in a pit and allowed to rot by mixing them with soil and water.

compost: decayed organic material used as a fertilizer for growing plants; **fertilizer**: a substance that is added to soil to help the growth of plants

Make Compost

Materials needed: Dry leaves, flowers, grass clippings, eggshells, fruit scraps, vegetable scraps, compost bin, shovel

1

A mixture of dry and wet waste materials and a good supply of air and water is necessary for composting. It is best carried out in the corner or on the edges of a garden. A compost is made either by digging a pit in the ground or in a bin.

2

Compost is built by adding dry and wet materials in layers. Begin by adding dry materials such as leaves and dry plants. Next, build a layer of wet materials such as green grass clippings, fruit scraps and vegetable scraps. Repeat the process till the bin or pit is full.

3

Sprinkle water over the pile. It is important that each layer is moist enough. However, too much water will drown the pile.

4

Stir all the layers well with the help of a shovel. Cover the pile with soil. If you are using a bin, cover it with a lid. Turn the materials in your compost once in a week.

5

It takes around a month for the compost to be ready. Then it can be fed to the garden.

What not to add: Cooked food, meat, fish, dairy products, ash, animal waste, used tissue papers

Observation: The compost becomes dry, brown and crumbly.

Conclusion: Tiny bacteria which are not visible to us, reduce the organic matter to compost.

Wrap up

* Leaves produce food and so they are known as food factories of plants.
* They have a pigment called chlorophyll that gives them the green colour.
* Most leaves have a leaf blade, leaf stalk, main vein and side veins.
* Leaves have different shapes, sizes, smell and textures.
* Leaves are of two types—simple and compound.
* Leaves are useful to us in many ways.
* Most trees shed their leaves once a year.

Brush up

A Give two examples of each.

1. Leaves with a distinct smell ....
2. Leaves which are used to make disposable plates ....
3. Leaves of these plants are of small size ....
4. Leaves that add flavour ....
5. Leaves that are eaten by us ....

B Fill in the blanks with the correct answers.

1. .... leaf is used for making medicines.
   a. Cactus b. Tulsi c. Lotus d. Croton
2. .... leaf is used for decoration.
   a. Rose b. Banana c. Mango d. Coriander
3. Chlorophyll allows plants to make food using ....
   a. water b. water, air and sunlight
   c. air and sunlight d. water and sunlight
4. The leaves of .... are used for dyeing.
   a. ashoka tree b. henna c. marigold d. methi

C Unscramble the following words with the help of the clues.

1. TIPEOEL (stalk of leaf) ....
2. TASOMTA (pores on the leaf) ....
3. MOCTSOP (natural fertilizer) ....

4. LCOOUR (red, yellow, green) ....

5. ROLPCHLOHYL (green pigment) ....

D Answer these questions.

1. What is a leaf blade?
2. How are leaves different from each other?
3. When do trees shed their leaves?
4. How are leaves useful? Write five points.
5. What should we remember not to add while making a compost pit?

Learn the ropes

Discuss the importance of a compost pit and try to make it.

Put your heads together

Form groups of four and collect leaves from the school compound or neighbourhood park. Classify each type of leaf and find out about them. Different groups can work on different leaf features—shape, size, texture, colour and smell, and on the uses of leaves. Note down your observations in a scrapbook.

Cross connect

Collect dried leaves, paste them on a chart paper and decorate to make cards or bookmarks.

4 Big and Small Animals

Get the ball rolling

Can you name these animals? Do all animals look the same? Which are the smallest and the biggest animals you have seen? Which animals have tails?

There are different kinds of animals that live around us. They are of different shapes and sizes. Big or small—each of them need food, water and shelter to survive. They live on land, in forests, in deserts, in water, on trees and under the ground.

Animals Around Us

The blue whale is the largest animal on Earth. It lives in water. On land, the African bush elephant is the largest, whereas the giraffe is the tallest animal. The ostrich is the largest bird.

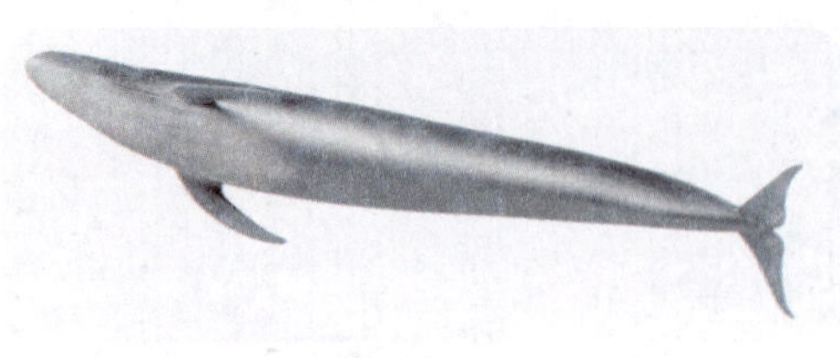
Blue whale

African bush elephant

Ostrich

Giraffe

Some big animals like tigers, bears, zebras, kangaroos, elephants, hippopotamus and rhinoceros live in forests. They are called **wild animals**.

Kangaroo

Hippopotamus

Bear

Shark

Sharks, dolphins and camels are also big animals. Do you know where they live?

Rabbit

Porcupine

Small animals like rabbits, porcupines and snakes also live in the wild. Other animals like dogs, cats, frogs, lizards and butterflies are small animals.

There are some animals that live with humans and are tamed. They are called **domestic animals**. Horses, cows, buffaloes, camels, sheep and goats are some domestic animals.

Sheep

Many animals like the giant panda, polar bear and penguins live only in specific regions where conditions are suitable for their survival.

Animal Bodies and Movements

Different animals have different bodies. Animals have different kinds of legs, wings, heart, bones, beaks, **feathers**, fur and **scales**. Some animals move with the help of their legs, some use wings to fly and some animals swim. Some animals do not have legs at all. Animals move from one place to another in search of food, shelter and to protect themselves from enemies.

Legs and feet

Animals move in different ways. They walk, run, **hop**, swim, fly, creep and crawl. All animals do not have four legs—some have four legs, some have six and some have eight. Elephants, camels, dogs and cats use their legs to walk. Tigers, leopards, cheetahs and horses run very fast using their legs. The cheetah is the fastest land animal.

Kangaroo

Cheetah

feathers: soft covering on a bird's body; **scales:** a flattened ridge plate forming part of the body covering of birds; **hop:** a short, quick jump

Rabbits and kangaroos hop on the ground. All these animals have four legs. Birds have two legs that help them **perch** on trees and walk and hop on the ground. Some animals like frogs, penguins and ducks have **webbed** feet that help them swim.

Penguin

Duck

Wings

Birds use their wings to move. They have two legs and two wings which are covered with feathers. Eagles, vultures and emus are **big birds**. Parrots, pigeons, sparrows and crows are **small birds**. Wings help birds to fly and move from one place to another. The bones of birds are **hollow**. Hence, they can easily lift their bodies for flight.

Sparrow

Emu

Tails and fins

Animals such as fish, whales and dolphins that live in water move with the help of **fins** and tails. They use their tail and fins to push through water.

Fish move with the help of fins

Give it a shot

List names of animals commonly found in your area. Take note of where they live, their body structure, whether they have a tail or not and how they use it.

Most animals have long or short tails, which are used for different purposes. Tigers, cheetahs and lions use their tails to balance themselves while making sharp turns when they run.

Animals like monkeys and chimpanzees which live on trees, can climb, hop and swing from one branch to another. Many animals also use their tails for brushing away flies and other insects from their bodies. Some animals like dogs wag their tail to show their feelings.

Chimpanzee

perch: to rest on something; **webbed**: having the toes connected by a thin fold of skin; **hollow:** having a hole or empty space inside; **fins**: a thin, vertical part sticking out of the body, especially of a fish

Muscles and scales

Underground animals such as snakes, slugs and earthworms do not have legs. They move by pushing their bodies along the ground using their muscles and scales. This kind of movement is called **creeping**. Animals like spiders, scorpions and ants walk slowly with their bodies close to the ground. This type of movement is called **crawling**.

Snake

Food Habits

Animals depend on plants and other animals for food. We know that different animals eat different kinds of food. Animals such as cows, goats, horses and deer feed only on plants and are known as **herbivores**. Animals which depend on other animals for food are called **carnivores**. Lions, panthers, crocodiles and tigers hunt smaller animals. Some carnivores such as hyenas, vultures and jackals do not hunt but feed on leftovers. These animals also feed on dead animals and are known as **scavengers**. Some animals eat both plants and other animals as food. They are known as **omnivores**. Crows, dogs and bears are omnivores.

A herd of deer

Clued in

The Japanese macaque eats a large variety of food including plants, insects and fruits. It is very picky with its food. It even washes its food before eating it.

Think through

Recycling helps us to make good use of our resources. In nature, there are many animals responsible for recycling. Who are they?

Some Uncommon Animals

There are many animals which are not commonly found. We see them at zoos and learn about them from books or the Internet. These animals are not found in other places on the Earth except in their region.

Dodo

Some animals lived a long time ago but are not alive anymore. They disappeared from Earth due to many reasons. Such animals are **extinct**. Some examples are dinosaurs and dodos. Animals that are in danger of becoming extinct are **endangered**. Some endangered animals are the giant panda, Bengal tiger and blue whale.

Dinosaur

Wrap up

* Animals are found everywhere and are both big and small.
* Animals can be wild or domesticated.
* They live in different places: on land, in forests, in deserts, in water, on trees and under the ground.
* Animals move from one place to another in search of food, shelter and to protect themselves from the enemies. They move in different ways.
* Different animals have different food habits.

Brush up

A Fill in the blanks with the correct answers.

1. Tigers, cheetahs and lions use their .... (tails/legs) to balance themselves while making sharp turns while running.
2. Dinosaurs lived long time ago but disappeared from Earth due to many reasons and are called .... (endangered/extinct).
3. Earthworms move by pushing their bodies along the ground as they do not have .... (muscles/legs).
4. The .... (body/bones) of birds are hollow hence, they can easily lift their bodies for flight.
5. Some animals like frogs and .... (eagles/penguins) have webbed feet that help them swim.

B Name them.

1. Largest bird ....
2. Tallest animal ....
3. Largest animal on the Earth ....
4. Largest animal living on land ....
5. Extinct animal ....

C Unscramble the names of these animals with the help of the clues.

1. KOMYEN (lives on trees) ....
2. FEGIRFA (tallest animal) ....

3. BRATIB (they hop on the ground) ....
4. NDLOIPHS (they live in water) ....
5. NASSKE (they do not have legs) ....

D Answer these questions.

1. What is the difference between herbivores and carnivores?
2. How do the tails of different animals help them?
3. What are scavengers?
4. What are the different ways in which animals move?
5. What are the food habits of different animals?

Learn the ropes

Make a poster on the theme, 'Scavengers help the environment'.

Put your heads together

Form five groups and choose an animal. Write a script on its life and enact it. Each group should choose a different animal. List five ways in which you can save them.

Cross connect

Find out the names of five animals which are not found in our country. Find out where they live. Learn the spellings of the names of the animals and the country they live in. Make an album and paste pictures of these animals in it.

5 Creepy Crawlies

Get the ball rolling

Do you know the name of this creepy crawly? Where have you seen it? Is it an insect? Why is it found in different places?

Among the animals that we see around us every day, which are the ones that scare you the most? Ants, grasshoppers, spiders, snails, worms, lizards and snails are some such animals.

Insects

Insects are small creatures that are found everywhere around us. They hide in corners inside our houses, in gardens, under the ground, on trees and in water. Some of them are useful to us, while some harm us. Common insects are ants, grasshoppers, cockroaches, mosquitoes, ladybirds and dragonflies.

Body of an insect

All insects have six legs. The body of an insect is divided into three parts—**head**, **thorax** and **abdomen**.

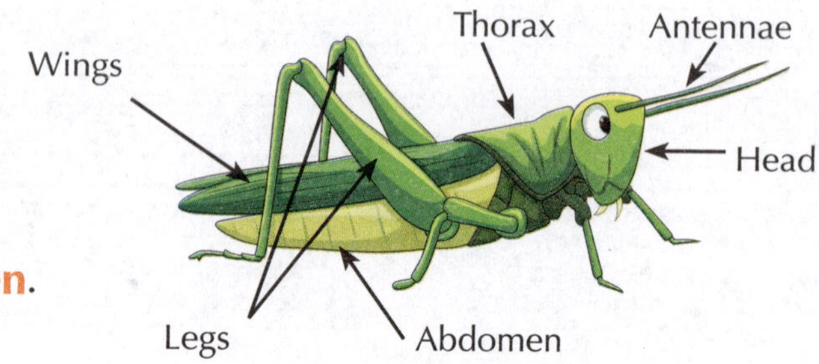

Body of a grasshopper

The head of an insect has two eyes, two **feelers** or **antennae** and a mouth. The antennae help the insects to smell, taste and hear. Insects have soft bodies and no bones but have a hard covering. The part of the insect's body between the neck and belly is the thorax.
The abdomen of an insect contains the heart and organs for breathing and digestion.

Some insects like flies have two wings. Beetles, dragonflies and bees have four wings. Insects like cockroaches, bees, wasps and beetles can walk as well as fly. Termites and ants generally crawl till they develop wings, after which they can fly as well. Mosquitoes and butterflies have wings that help them fly. Insects like silverfish and louse do not have wings and can only crawl.

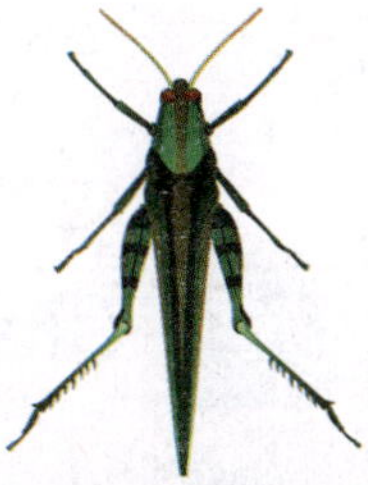
Grasshopper

Butterfly

Silverfish

Insects have a special type of mouth which helps them to get their food. Butterflies use their tube-like mouth to suck nectar from flowers. Mosquitoes suck blood with its needle-like mouth. Grasshoppers have a biting and chewing type of mouth with which they feed on plant parts.

Beetle

Cockroach

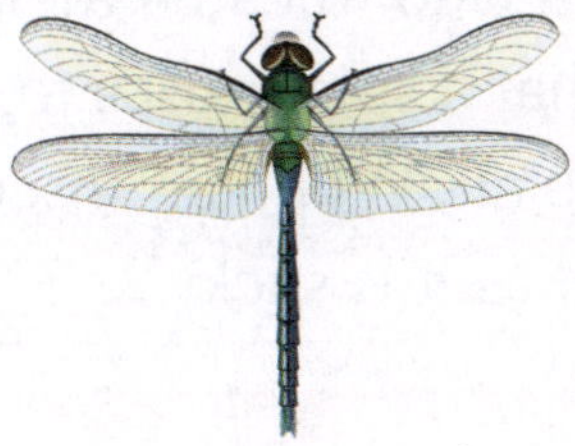
Dragonfly

Worms and Snails

Worms and snails are common sights in our gardens. While worms can be seen **squirming** on the ground, snails are seen crawling across leaves and on plant stems. Both are known to be wriggly and slimy. Snails have very soft bodies and no bones. Snails have a hard, round shell on their bodies that protects them.

Snail

Worms are soft-bodied. They have a long **cylindrical** tube-like body and no limbs. Earthworms cannot fly, they **wriggle** and crawl. Centipedes, millipedes and caterpillars have many legs. Caterpillars are the young ones of butterflies.

Centipede

Caterpillar

Earthworm

squirming: wriggle or twist the body from side to side; **cylindrical:** shaped like a cylinder; **wriggle**: twist and turn

Reptiles

Lizards, garden lizards and chameleons are all reptiles. Lizards have a long sticky tongue which helps them catch their food. Most of the reptiles feed on insects like mosquitoes, butterflies, moth, house flies and cockroaches.

Lizard

Chameleon

Chameleons usually eat large insects such as locusts, grasshoppers, crickets and stick insects. They change their colour according to their surroundings so that they can hide from their enemies. This is called **camouflaging**.

Spiders

Spiders are neither insects nor worms. They are not reptiles either. Their body is divided into two parts and they have eight legs. Spiders are of different types and are found almost everywhere. They are found in corners of rooms and in dark areas of cupboards. Some spiders also live on plants and trees.

Spider in its web

Clued in

Most spiders have eight eyes. Spiders also have tiny hair on their legs which help them hear and smell.

Spiders spin a web to catch their prey. They **secrete** a liquid that forms a sticky thread. This thread that a spider uses to make its web comes out of its body as liquid, but dries quickly in the air. When an insect such as a mosquito flies into a spider's web, it gets stuck on the thread as it is sticky.

Give it a shot

List the names of creepy crawlies that you see around you under the given headings.

Insects	Worms	Reptiles	Spiders

camouflaging: to hide oneself by changing colour so that they cannot be seen against their surroundings;
secrete: to produce a liquid substance

Useful Creepy Crawlies

Creepy crawlies are useful to us in many ways.

- Earthworms mix up the soil. Their digging loosens the soil and makes it fertile.
- Honeybees give us honey.
- Silkworms give us silk, which is used to make clothes.
- Lizards help us by eating flies and mosquitoes, which helps in preventing diseases caused by them.

Harmful Creepy Crawlies

Mosquito

Some creepy crawlies are harmful to us. Bee and wasp stings can be painful. They use a body part called **sting** to defend themselves when attacked. Flies spread diseases such as cholera, food poisoning and diarrhoea. They sit on garbage and dirt, and transfer the germs sticking to their bodies to our food. When we eat this food, we fall sick.

Mosquitoes bite humans and cause diseases like malaria, dengue and chikungunya. Mosquitoes breed in **stagnant** water. We should keep our surroundings clean and not allow water to collect near our homes or in containers.

Think through

Tithi found some tiny animals in her garden. How will she know which of those tiny animals are insects?

Wrap up

- Creepy crawlies can be insects, worms, snails, lizards or spiders.
- An insect's body can be divided into the head, thorax and abdomen.
- Earthworms and snails have soft bodies and no bones.
- Lizards, chameleons and garden lizards are reptiles.
- Spiders are neither insects, nor worms, nor are they reptiles.
- Some creepy crawlies are helpful, while some are harmful.

Brush up

A Who am I?

1. I spin a web and people think I am an insect, which I am not. ....

stagnant: still or motionless

2. I suck blood with my needle-like mouth. ....

3. I change my colour according to the surroundings. ....

4. I am slimy, do not have bones but have a hard-round shell. ....

B Give one example of each.

1. Insect with four wings ....
2. Insect that can sting ....
3. Insect that can fly ....
4. Insect that causes diseases ....

C Write T for true and F for false.

1. Silkworms give us silk, which is used to make clothes. ☐
2. Lizards mix up the soil and make it fertile. ☐
3. Worms and snails are wriggly and slimy. ☐
4. Silverfish love to swim in water. ☐

D Answer these questions.

1. Write two special features of insects.
2. Name the body parts of an insect.
3. What is camouflaging?
4. Explain three ways each in which creepy crawlies can be helpful and harmful to us.
5. How does a spider make a web?

Learn the ropes

How do earthworms and beetles make the soil better? How do you think you can make sure that they do not get harmed?

Put your heads together

Divide the class into two groups. One group will work on flies and the other group on mosquitoes. Each group has to find out the diseases caused by them, how it spreads, and how to prevent it. Then, enter all the information in a scrapbook. Make a poster about the information you have collected and write a slogan too.

Cross connect

A. Make a comic strip where one of the creepy crawlies is the main character.

B. Make a paper butterfly. You will need a toilet roll, glue and coloured paper.

1. Wrap a toilet roll with coloured paper.
2. Make cut-outs of butterfly wings from another sheet of coloured paper (of a different colour).
3. Design the butterfly wings to make it colourful and bright.
4. Paste the wings on the back of the toilet roll.
5. Make cut-outs of a butterfly's feelers and paste them on top of the toilet roll.
6. Take a pen and draw the face of the butterfly. Your paper butterfly is ready!

6 Birds

Get the ball rolling

Name the birds you see around your area. What are the different sounds they make? Are they saying something to each other? Do you feed any birds or keep water for them?

Birds are animals whose bodies are covered with feathers. They live on land, on trees and near seas or freshwater bodies. Birds have a pair of wings and feet. Some commonly seen birds are crows, sparrows, hens, doves, pigeons and eagles. Almost all birds can fly. Some of us think that any animal that has wings is a bird. Bats and flies have wings and can fly but they are not birds.

Crow

Dove

Features of Birds

The body of a bird is divided into three parts—**head**, **trunk** and **tail**. They have two pairs of limbs—wings towards the front and legs at the back. They do not have hands. Birds have two eyes, one beak and no teeth. They have different

Parts of a bird's body

types of legs with sharp claws. They use their claws to perch on branches, scratch the ground and hold their food. Birds build nests and lay eggs.

Wings

Birds have special **features** that help them fly. They fly with the help of wings that are attached to their bodies by strong **flight muscles**. These muscles help them move their wings up and down. Wings are covered with feathers. Birds have a boat-shaped (**streamlined**) body which helps them fly easily in the air. Their bones are hollow, which makes them light.

Ostrich

Kiwi

Eagle

Although, all birds have wings and feathers, they fly at different heights and cover different distances. Birds like cranes, red knots and parrots fly long distances. Peacocks and hens fly short distances. Eagles, white storks and vultures fly very high in the sky. Sparrows, pelicans and bulbuls fly low. Not all birds that have wings and feathers can fly. Some birds such as the kiwi, penguin, emu and ostrich cannot fly as they have heavy bodies and weak flight muscles.

Pelican

Feathers

The body of a bird is covered with feathers, which give shape, make the bird colourful and help it fly. Feathers are of three types—body feathers, down feathers and flight feathers.

Think through

Why should we never keep birds in cages?

Body feathers cover the body to give it shape.

Down feathers are small, soft and fluffy feathers that cover their bodies. Very young birds are covered only in down feathers, which trap the body heat and keep them warm.

Peacocks have colourful feathers

Flight feathers help the birds to fly. They are present in wings and tails of birds and help them change their direction while flying. Feathers also help birds to swim. The feathers of some **aquatic** birds are waterproof which prevents them from getting wet. Ducks and penguins have such feathers. The colourful feathers give birds a distinct look and also help them hide from enemies.

Flight feather

Down feather

features: a quality or important part of something; **streamlined**: to shape something so that it can move as quickly as possible through air and water; **aquatic**: living or growing in water

Beaks

Hummingbird's beak

Sparrow's beak

Duck's beak

Birds use their beaks to catch and eat food. Beaks are of different shapes depending on the kind of food birds eat. Sparrows have strong beaks so that they can crack open the nuts and seeds that they eat. Hummingbirds and sunbirds have long, narrow, pointed and straw-like beaks that help them suck nectar from flowers. Ducks have broad and flat beaks with holes on either side to drain out the water leaving the worms, insects and plants in their mouth. Birds use their beaks for gathering materials that are used for making nests. They also use their beaks for cleaning their feathers and feeding their young ones.

Birds use beaks to feed their young ones

Feet

Birds' feet are of different sizes and shapes. They have two feet with four toes, three of which face forward and one backwards. Feet are used to walk, hop, hold and catch preys and pick things.

Crow's feet

Some birds like crows, sparrows and mynahs perch on the branches of trees. They have toes that help them to grip and hold branches firmly.

Birds like hens have sharp and hard claws to scratch the ground and dig out insects and grains.

Eagle's feet

Birds like eagles and hawks have strong, sharp, large and curved claws known as **talons**.

Woodpeckers have feet and toes that help them cling to tree trunks and climb up.

Duck's feet

Aquatic birds like ducks and swans have webbed feet that help them swim.

Some birds like ostrich have two toes instead of four, which they use for running.

Birds and Their Sounds

Birds use their tongue to chirp as a way of communicating. The sounds are of two kinds—**call** and **song**. A call or a chirp is made to warn others of danger so that they can protect themselves. A song is a sound which is **musical**. Cuckoos and nightingales make such sounds. Parrots can **mimic** human sounds and can speak like us.

Nests

Birds make nests to lay eggs. They use different materials like grass, straw, thread, wool, twigs and strips of cloth to make their nest. They use their beaks to collect these things and build their nests. They hatch their eggs by keeping them warm in the nest. Once the baby birds are strong enough to fly, they leave their nests.

Clued in

Unlike most birds that sing, a woodpecker drums its beak against a tree. Other woodpeckers can identify which bird it is by the sound of the drumming.

Different types of birds live in different places depending on the climate of the place. However, there are some birds that travel long distances to escape cold weather, in search of food and to lay eggs. When the season changes, they return to the place where they belong. This is known as **migration**. Birds that migrate are known as **migratory birds**.

Nest

Caring for Birds

Bird feeding is an activity of feeding wild birds, often by means of a **bird feeder**. Food items like peanuts, grain, seeds, kitchen scraps and water in bowls can be kept in open spaces in the garden or in our balconies.

Give it a shot

Name at least five birds you commonly see in your locality. Observe them and note down these points—how they look, where they live, what they eat, and what sound they make. Draw or paste their pictures too.

Wrap up

- Birds live on land and near the sea and freshwater bodies.
- Birds have wings and feathers but they fly at different heights and over different distances.
- Some birds cannot fly as they have heavy bodies and weak flight muscles.
- The body of a bird is covered with feathers, which give shape, make the bird colourful and help it to fly.

musical: (of a sound) pleasant to listen to; **mimic:** to copy the way somebody speaks, moves or behaves; **migration**: movement from one region to another and often back again, especially according to the season of the year

* Birds have beaks which they use to eat food, gather materials that are used for making nests, to clean their feathers and feed their young ones.
* Birds' feet are of different sizes and shapes.
* Birds use their tongue to chirp. It is their way of communicating with each other.
* Birds that travel long distances to escape from cold conditions in search of food and to lay eggs are known as migratory birds.

Brush up

A Identify the claws and write the names of the birds they belong to.

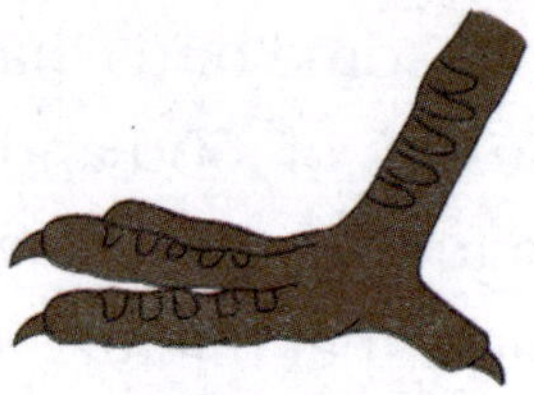

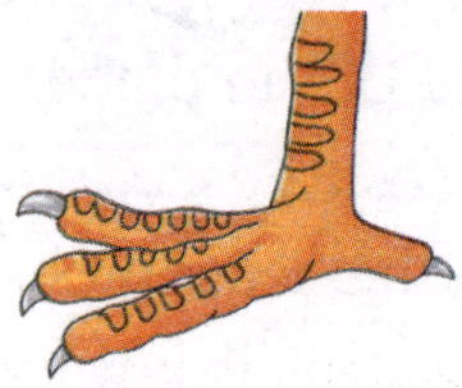

1. .... 2. ....
3. ....

B Fill in the blanks.

1. The body of a bird is divided into the head, ... and tail.
2. The feathers of some birds are ....
3. .... have toes which help them to grip and hold the branch firmly.
4. Birds .... to warn others of danger so that they can protect themselves.
5. Birds use their .... to chirp.

C Write T for true or F for false.

1. Any animal which has wings is a bird. ☐
2. All birds can fly. ☐
3. Birds use their beaks to catch and eat food. ☐
4. Birds leave their nest once the baby birds are strong enough to fly. ☐
5. People should keep birds in cages and feed them. ☐

D Answer these questions.

1. Why do birds build nests?
2. What is the difference between a down feather and a flight feather?
3. What are the special features that help birds to fly?
4. Why do birds migrate?
5. How do birds communicate?

Learn the ropes

Make a bird feeder and water bath using mud bowls or any open container. A feeder bowl can be filled with grains, nuts and seeds. Remember to replace the food and water when it gets dirty. Note how many kinds of birds visit your garden or balcony. Identify them, collect their pictures or draw them.

Put your heads together

Form five groups. Each group can choose their favourite bird. On a chart, write down their colour, size, type of claws, feeding habits and sounds. Draw or paste their pictures along with this information.

Cross connect

Collect feathers from the gardens, parks or other open places. Paste them and draw the bird it belongs to next to them.

7 Children at Work

Get the ball rolling

Have you seen people doing different kinds of work around you? What kinds of work do they do? Do you help your parents at home with the housework?

People need to work to earn money so that they can get the basic things they need in life. The work that people do to earn money is their **job** or **occupation**.

Types of Work

People have different kinds of jobs. They work at home, in an office, on a farm or at a school. A postman, plumber, carpenter, doctor, school teacher, house helper, nurse and bus driver are examples of different kinds of people who help us. Every job is equally important and we should respect all jobs.

Teacher

Give it a shot

Look at the pictures and write the occupations of these people.

1. .... 2. .... 3. .... 4. .... 5. ....

Working at Home

At home, family members work together and help each other. Our parents go to work so that they can provide things for us. At home, they do the **household** work, buy things needed at home, help their children with the studies and take care of family members when they fall ill.

Our grandparents take care of us

Some families are big families, where the grandparents may also help with the housework. They look after the children and sometimes even pick and drop the children from the school bus stop. They also help the children with their studies.

Some parents employ a helper who does the household work and takes care of the children as well.

All members of a family must share the **responsibilities** of housework. Children should also help their family with tasks at home. These can be tidying up the bedroom, packing school bags, laying the table for dinner and helping in carrying the dishes from the table after meals. They can also help in simple tasks like watering the plants and keeping their clothes in their cupboard. A family in which members help each other is a happy family.

Think through

What do you think would happen if there was no one to drive our school bus or deliver our courier packages?

household: connected with a house or flat and the people living in it; **responsibility:** a duty to deal with or take care of somebody/something

Children at Work

10 REDUCED INEQUALITIES

There are many people in our country who are poor. They do not have enough money for their daily needs and certainly not enough left to send their children to school. In such families, the children too need to take up a job or some kind of work to earn money for the family. In some cases, children work in the morning and do odd jobs such as cleaning people's cars, ironing clothes, selling tea, delivering newspapers and milk to homes. Some of them also attend school in the afternoon.

Child working at a tea stall

There are others who work all day at tea stalls or *dhabas*, as domestic help in houses, in factories that make clothes or firecrackers, in **mines** or as street hawkers selling things on the road to earn money. These children cannot go to school at all. When children are **employed** to work for money, it is called **child labour**. These children work in unhealthy conditions, which can be harmful for their health. They work for long hours and are not paid as much as an adult for the same kind of work.

Preventing Child Labour

Every child has the right to study and play. Child labour is a problem that is present all over the world. In India, it is illegal to employ a child below the age of 14 years. However, there are such children all over our country. It is important to find ways to stop this. There are many organizations like CRY (Child Rights and You), UNICEF (United Nations International Children's Emergency Fund) and the Kailash Satyarthi Children's Foundation that work towards putting an end to child labour and make the world child-friendly.

Child labour

Clued in

Under the Right to Education Act, it is **compulsory** for every child, 14 years and below, to attend school. The Act helps poor children to go to school without their parents having to spend money on their school fees, uniform, books and bags. The midday meal scheme in government schools was started so that the children coming to these schools would not be hungry.

mine: a big hole made deep in the Earth to dig out materials like coal, gold and diamonds; **employed**: give regular work to a person and pay them for the work; **compulsory**: something that has to be done

Wrap up

- People do different kinds of jobs to earn money.
- In a family too, all members work, but in different ways.
- It is important for all members to do the household work.
- When children are employed to work for money, it is called child labour.
- In India, under the Right to Education Act, every child must go to school.
- There are many organizations in India that are working for children's rights.

Brush up

A Answer in one word.

1. Work that people do to earn money ....
2. Places where children work ....
3. A type of factory where children work ....
4. This act protects the children's rights to go to school ....
5. This organization fights against child labour ....

B Write T for true or F for false.

1. Only mothers look after the needs of the family. ☐
2. Only some jobs are important. ☐
3. Children must not help at home. ☐
4. Some children work as well as study. ☐
5. Children under the age of 14 can be employed in factories and mines. ☐

C Fill in the blanks.

1. All members of a family should help with the ....
2. Doing a job to earn money is called ....
3. Children earning for money is part of child ....
4. .... is an organization that works for child rights.
5. Under the .... Act, all children must go to school.

D Answer these questions.

1. What is the meaning of the word 'occupation'?
2. List five examples of occupations of people you know.
3. What are the different ways in which you help your family at home?
4. What is child labour? Why is it harmful for children?
5. Why is it important for all children to be educated?

Learn the ropes

Every work is important and we should respect all kinds of work and the people doing that work. Think of all those people who are not your family and are not related to you but still work to make your life comfortable. Make a list of these people and write in what way will you show respect to them.

Put your heads together

We should encourage working children to go to school. In groups, make a list of the things you can do to make this possible. An example is donating textbooks or pencil boxes.

Cross connect

Make a 'Thank You' card for all people who work at your home or in school. They could be people such as helpers, gardeners or the school guard. Write a few lines about the things they do to make your life easy and gift the card to them.

8 The Games We Play

Get the ball rolling

Do you go to the park to play with your friends? What games do you play in school during the games period? Do you watch any sport on TV? Which is your favourite sport?

We like to do many things in our free time like playing games on computers or mobile phones, cycling, playing football or listening to music. This free time, when we do not study or do school-related work and instead do something we enjoy is called **leisure**. The activity that we do in our spare or leisure time is called **recreation**. We play games for leisure and recreation.

Cycling

Listening to music

Playing games is a good way to spend our leisure time. It is an enjoyable way of exercising and keeps us active and full of energy. There are different types of games that children play. These can be **indoor games** or **outdoor games**.

Think through

There is an old saying, 'All work and no play makes Jack a dull boy.' What do you think this means?

Indoor Games

Games that we play inside our houses, classrooms or school buildings are called indoor games. Some indoor games are card games like Uno™ and **boardgames** such as chess, carrom, ludo and Monopoly™. We also play table top games like billiards, snooker and table tennis. Nowadays, we play games on computers, **tablets** and mobile phones. Some of us also play games on special machines called PlayStation™ and Xbox™. Some of us also play with electronic toys.

We play games on computers

Board games

Table tennis

Carrom

Outdoor Games

Games played outside in open areas such as a park, a field or in a special area like a **court** are known as outdoor games. Some popular outdoor games are cricket, football, basketball, hockey, volleyball, cycling, tennis, badminton and roller skating. Outdoor games also include **athletics**. Outdoor games keep us healthy as they are a good way to exercise. They are good for both mind and body.

Basketball

Cricket

Football

Volleyball

Break time or the games period in school is a favourite time for us as we get to play our favourite games with our friends.

Individual and Team Games

Indoor and outdoor games can be played either by a single person or by many players together. These are **individual games** and **team games**. In an individual game, only one player is needed to play the game. Some individual games are swimming, running and archery.

Clued in

Mithali Dorai Raj, captain of the Indian women's cricket team, is the only female to surpass 6000+ runs mark in one-day matches.

boardgames: games played on a board often using a dice and other pieces; **tablet**: a small computer that is usually controlled by means of a touch screen; **athletics**: sports such as running, jumping and throwing that people compete in

Football, cricket, basketball and volleyball are some team games. Playing team games is important as it teaches us cooperation and teamwork. Some schools have sports coaches who train the students in team games.

Games in the Past

When our grandparents were children, there were no televisions, computers, tablets or mobile phones. Our grandparents in those days spent most of their leisure time playing outdoor games with friends, cousins and other family members.

The games played in the past were different. Children in those days played hopscotch, *gilli danda*, seven tiles or *pitthoo*, kabaddi, hide and seek, *langri taang*, *kancha* or marbles, lock and key, kho kho and kite flying. Skipping rope, playing with the hula hoop and *keekli* were also enjoyed. These were simple games that did not need expensive toys or devices and involved teamwork and cooperation.

Kabaddi

Marbles

Seven tiles (pitthoo)

When Games Become Work

A game in which players are trained and is played for competition is called a **sport**. A person who plays a sport is called a **sportsperson**. However, a person whose occupation is to play a sport for money is called a **professional player**.

Some sports that are played for money by professionals are cricket, football, hockey, badminton, wrestling, weightlifting, boxing, athletics, archery, polo, snooker, billiards and chess.

Games play an important role in maintaining a healthy mind, body and soul. Playing games is an essential part of growing up and being with friends. They not only develop physical fitness but also teach obedience, discipline, patience, presence of mind and accepting defeat in the right way.

Give it a shot

Which is your favourite outdoor sport? Find the name of a famous professional player of that sport and get his or her picture. Find out some more information about him or her. Make a scrapbook on the player.

professional: a person who does a job for a salary

Professional Players

Sachin Tendulkar

Sachin Tendulkar started playing cricket at the age of 11. He is the only player to complete more than 30,000 runs in international cricket. Tendulkar is the youngest and the first sportsperson to receive the Bharat Ratna, India's highest civilian award.

Saina Nehwal

Saina Nehwal won the gold medal at the 2018 Commonwealth Games. She has won more than 23 international titles. She won the bronze medal at the 2012 London Olympics becoming the first Indian badminton player to win a medal at the Olympics. She is also the first Indian to win the Australian Super Series. She received the Padma Bhushan in 2016.

Mary Kom

Chungneijang Mary Kom Hmangte, popularly known as Mary Kom, is an Indian boxer from Manipur. She is a six time World Amateur Boxing Champion and the only woman boxer to win a medal in each of the seven world championships. Nicknamed 'Magnificent Mary', she is the only Indian woman boxer who qualified for the 2012 Summer Olympics. She is the first Indian woman boxer to win the gold medal at the Asian Games in 2014 in South Korea and she is also the first Indian woman boxer to get the gold medal at the 2018 Commonwealth Games.

Sushil Kumar Solanki

Sushil Kumar is a freestyle wrestler and won the silver medal at the 2012 London Olympics. He also won the gold medal in the 2014 Commonwealth Games. He received the Rajiv Gandhi Khel Ratna, India's highest honour for sports persons in 2009.

Sania Mirza

Sania Mirza is an Indian professional tennis player who has won 6 Grand Slam titles in her career and was ranked as India's number one singles player up till her retirement in 2013. She is the highest-ranked female player ever from India. She has also won a total of 14 medals (including 6 Gold) at three major multi-sport events, namely the Asian Games, the Commonwealth Games and the Afro-Asian Games.

Viswanathan Anand

Viswanathan Anand is an Indian chess grandmaster and a former world chess champion. Also known as 'Vishy' and 'Tiger of Madras', Anand was awarded the prestigious Padma Shri at an early age of 18. Later in 2017, he was also awarded the highly acclaimed Padma Vibhushan, India's second highest civilian award. He won the World Rapid Chess champion in 2003 and 2017.

Wrap up

* Playing games is as important as studying.
* Games can either be played indoors or outdoors.
* In the past, games were mostly played outdoors and did not require any expensive equipment.
* A game in which players get training and is played for competition is a sport.
* Players who play for money are known as professional players.

Brush up

A Fill in the blanks.

1. Games which are played inside are known as .... games.
2. Cricket and cycling are .... games.
3. Both indoor and outdoor games can be played with a .... player or with .... players.
4. Swimming and running are examples of .... player games.
5. People whose occupation is to play a sport are .... players.

B Write T for true and F for false.

1. Chess is an outdoor game. ☐
2. Our grandparents played with PlayStation™ when they were young. ☐
3. Virat Kohli is a professional cricketer. ☐
4. Computers, tablets and mobile phones are used nowadays to play games. ☐
5. Games should be played according to the rules. ☐

C Match the sport with the personalities.

1. Cricket	a. Mary Kom
2. Wrestling	b. Sushil Kumar Solanki
3. Badminton	c. Sachin Tendulkar
4. Boxing	d. Saina Nehwal

D Answer these questions.

1. Why should we play games?
2. How are games of the past different from the games played nowadays?
3. Differentiate between games and sports.
4. Who are professional players? Write the names of two professional players and the sport they play.
5. What are indoor and outdoor games?

Learn the ropes

Your school is holding its inter-section cricket matches for class 3. It is the last match today that will decide whether your section wins or loses. It looks like your team is going to lose. Some of your classmates decide to cheat so that your section can win. Is it right to cheat even if it is in a game? What will you do?

Put your heads together

What do you do with the toys you no longer want to play with? Are they just lying around in your room or piled up in your cupboard? In groups, think of some interesting ideas to reuse your old toys and make something new from them.

Cross connect

India has an old tradition of making toys. Each region in India has different types of toys and dolls made from cloth, mud, bamboo and even metal. These are called folk toys. Punjab is famous for toys made of cloth and Rajasthan for its puppets. Find out the traditional folk toys of the state you are living in and make a presentation on it in the classroom.

9 Food We Eat

Get the ball rolling

What is your favourite food? Do you know the names of all the food items on the table in these pictures? Where do these food items come from?

All living things need energy. We get energy from the food we eat. We get food either from plants or from animals.

Food from Plants

We get fruits, vegetables, nuts, grains, cereals and pulses from plants. We also get herbs and spices from plants. Different parts of plants are eaten as food.

Carrot, radish, beetroot and turnip are **roots** of plants.

Ginger, onion and garlic are **stems** of plants.

Carrots

Ginger

Garlic

Onion

Cabbage, lettuce, spinach, coriander (*dhania*), mint and fenugreek (*methi*) are **leaves** of plants. Cauliflower and broccoli are **flowers** of plants. Peas and pulses such as moong, *urad* and *chana* are **seeds** of plants. **Cereals** such as rice, wheat and bajra are also seeds of plants. We get sugar from the sugarcane **stem**, coffee from coffee beans and tea from tea **leaves**.

Broccoli

Fenugreek

Sugarcane

Spices

Spices add **aroma** and taste to the food. We get spices such as pepper, clove, cinnamon, cardamom, turmeric and cumin from plants.

Oil is important as it is needed to cook food. We get vegetable oil from the seeds of plants such as groundnut, sunflower, coconut and mustard.

Guava

Pineapple

We eat fruits of many plants. Apple, banana, pineapple, guava and papaya are examples of some fruits. These fruits are eaten raw. Some fruits can also be cooked and eaten. Most vegetables like pumpkin, gourd, bitter gourd, brinjal are cooked and eaten. Cucumbers and carrots are eaten raw in salads.

Food from Animals

We get different kinds of food from animals. Most of them are cooked before eating. Animals like cows, goats and buffaloes give us milk. In mountains, milk is obtained from sheep and yaks. In hot regions and deserts, people get milk from camels. Milk is used to make paneer, curd, cheese, butter and ghee. These are known as **milk products**. Hens, ducks and geese give us eggs.

Eggs

Milk products

We eat different kinds of fish like rohu, pomfret, mackerel and sardines. Some people

Sardines

Pomfret

cereals: grains or seeds like maize, wheat and rice; **aroma**: a strong, pleasant smell eat **seafood** like prawns, lobsters and oysters. We get meat from hens and goats. Honey is made from the nectar of flowers by honeybees.

People who eat plants and milk products are known as **vegetarians**. People who eat egg, fish and meat along with milk products and plants are called **non-vegetarians**.

Food is very important for our bodies. It gives us energy to walk, run and play. The energy we get from food is used for different activities by the body. Food helps us to grow and protects us from diseases.

Kinds of Food

There are different kinds of food items. These food items can be listed into three major food groups; **energy-giving food**, **body-building food** and **protective foods**.

Energy-giving food

Food that gives us energy is called **energy giving food**. Rice, wheat, sugar, potato and bread are rich in **carbohydrates**. They give energy to the body. Food such as butter, oil and ghee are rich in **fats**. Fats provide energy and warmth to the body.

Rice

Potato

Bread

Body-building food

Body-building food helps our body to grow as they are rich in **proteins**. Eggs, milk, meat, fish, paneer, cheese, soybean and pulses are rich in proteins. Proteins are important for growth and repair of the body.

Paneer

Soybean

Protective food

Protective food like fruits, vegetables and milk give us **vitamins** and **minerals**. They help us to stay healthy by protecting the body from diseases. Carbohydrates, fats, proteins, vitamins and minerals are called **nutrients**. The food we eat should have all the nutrients to help us work, grow and stay healthy.

Fruits and vegetables

Clued in

Milk is a complete food. It contains carbohydrates, proteins, fats, calcium (mineral) and vitamins.

How We Get Food

A vegetable vendor

Food travels a long journey before it reaches our homes or plates. Plants are grown by farmers. They sow crops and **harvest** them when they ripen. The **produce** is then sold in a *mandi* or a wholesale market. Shopkeepers and vendors buy the produce from the mandi. We buy fruits and vegetables from shopkeepers or vendors.

Food we get from animals comes from farms. Hens and ducks are raised in **poultry farms**. Meat and eggs are sent to the market from poultries. Cows and buffaloes are raised in **dairy farms**. We get milk from milk booths, shops and even dairies. Shopkeepers buy milk directly from dairies. Butter, cheese and ice creams are made, processed and packaged at factories.

Give it a shot

Write down the names of food you eat each day for three days. Put a tick or a cross in each column, depending on the kind of food you have eaten. Observe the table carefully and notice the type of food you eat more and the type of food you eat less. How will you balance your meals to get all the nutrients important for your body?

	Food Item	Energy-giving food	Body-building food	Protective food
Day 1				
Day 2				
Day 3				

Cultural Diversity in Food

Think through

Find out the most common food items eaten in Kashmir, Uttarakhand, Meghalaya and Madhya Pradesh.

The type of food one eats depends on the region where one lives, the climate, local customs, habits and availability of the food items. *Makki di roti* and *sarson da saag* are popular dishes in north India. People living in the coastal areas eat a lot of seafood like fish and prawns. Idli, dosa, sambar and coconut chutney are eaten widely in south India. *Dal baati* and *gatte ki sabzi* are popular dishes of Rajasthan. In some regions of India, spicy food is eaten. In some regions, **bland** food is preferred. Some people like perfectly-cooked food, while some people like semi-cooked food. The same food can be prepared differently as per the taste of people.

Dal baati

harvest: the process of gathering plants that are ready to be used; **produce**: freshly harvested crops; **poultry farms**: farms on which chickens are raised for their eggs or meat; **dairy farms**: farms on which milk and milk products are produced; **bland**: not having strong flavour

Wrap up

- Living things need energy to live. We get energy from the food we eat.
- We get food either from plants or from animals.
- Food gives us energy, helps us grow and protects us from diseases.
- Food travels a long journey before it reaches our homes or our plates.
- The type of food one eats depends on the region one lives in its climate, local customs and habits.
- People in different parts of the world eat different kinds of food.

Brush up

A Give two examples of each.

1. Body-building food ....
2. Protective food ....
3. Energy-giving food ....
4. Vegetarian food ....
5. Non-vegetarian food ....

B Write T for true and F for false.

1. We get honey from plants. ☐
2. Non-vegetarians eat only plants and milk products. ☐
3. Wheat and rice are cereals. ☐
4. We depend on plants and animals for food. ☐
5. We get milk from poultry farms. ☐

C Fill in the blanks.

1. The energy we get from food is used for different .... of the body.
2. Some vegetables like .... and .... are eaten raw as salads.

3. Fruits and vegetables give us .... and ....
4. People living in the coastal areas eat a lot of ....

D Answer these questions.

1. Name the different parts of a plant that we eat.
2. What are spices and why do we use them? Give some examples.
3. What is the difference between vegetarians and non-vegetarians?
4. What is protective food? Explain with the help of examples.
5. How does food from plants reach our homes?

Learn the ropes

Vivan met with an accident and fractured his ankle. What kind of food should he eat and why?

Put your heads together

Work in groups. Ask an elder at home to give you the spices that are used the most in everyday food. Place the spices in plastic bags separately. Bring them to the class and stick the packets on a chart paper. Write the names of these spices as we know them in Hindi, English or any other language you know. Share your chart in class.

Cross connect

Every family has a favourite recipe. Ask our parents to teach you a simple recipe that you can make with them. Remember to write the recipe step-by-step. Decorate your recipe with the list of items you require.

10 Cooking

Get the ball rolling

Have you ever helped your mother in cooking? What did you cook and how? What do you eat that is not cooked? What is eaten only when cooked?

Cucumber is eaten raw

Ladies' finger is cooked and eaten

All of us need food to stay fit and healthy. Early humans ate raw food because they did not know how to cook. Human beings started cooking food after the discovery of fire. However, not all food items need to be cooked. Vegetables such as cucumber, radish and carrot can be eaten raw. Vegetables such as ladies' finger (okra), potato and gourd need to be cooked. Cooking makes food soft, tasty and easy to chew and **digest**. It also kills **germs** present in the food. People use different methods for cooking a variety of dishes.

Cooking With Water

We cook food in many ways. In some methods of cooking, water is used. In some methods, food can be cooked without water.

digest: when food is broken down by the body; **germs:** very small organisms that cause diseases

Boiling

Boiling rice

Boiling is one of the simplest method of cooking. The food item along with water is placed in a pan or a **wok** and boiled. Rice, pulses, vegetables and eggs are cooked by boiling. Milk is boiled to kill germs present in it.

Steaming

Idli in a steamer

Food can be steamed in a pressure cooker or a **steamer**. Water is poured in a utensil and boiled. The steam which rises from the boiling water cooks the food. Dhoklas, idlis and momos are cooked by steaming. Steaming food is the best method of cooking as the nutrients are not lost. Steamed food is healthy because no oil is used.

Cooking Without Water

Food is cooked without water by frying, baking, grilling and roasting the ingredients.

Frying

Frying

Frying is a method of cooking food in hot oil or ghee. When food is completely soaked in hot oil or ghee in a pan, it is called **deep frying**. Poori, samosa, pakoras and chips are cooked by deep frying. When food is cooked in less oil, it is called **shallow frying**. Parathas, cutlets, pancakes and omelettes are cooked by shallow frying. Food cooked rapidly over a high heat while stirring fast is called **stir-frying**. Fried food contains a lot of oil and should be eaten in less quantities.

Baking

In baking, food is cooked in an oven or a microwave oven. Food is heated for a long time without exposing it directly to flames. Breads, cakes and biscuits are made by baking.

Baking

Clued in

A small dish of water placed in an oven prevents the crust of bread from becoming too hard or brown.

wok: a large pan-shaped like bowl; **steamer**: a metal container with small holes in it, which is placed over a pan of boiling water to cook food in the steam

Grilling

Grilling

In this method of cooking, food is cooked on a **metal grill**. Heat is applied to the food by placing heated charcoal under the grill. Sometimes a **grill pan** can be used to grill food. This method of cooking is used to cook meat and vegetables quickly. Meat, paneer and sandwiches are usually grilled.

Roasting

Roasting

Food is roasted by cooking it over a fire or in an oven. Hot air envelops the food and cooks it evenly on all sides. Meat, fish, vegetables, chapattis and dry fruits are cooked by roasting.

Vessels for Cooking

Vessels used for cooking food are known as **cooking vessels** or **cooking utensils**. They are made of different materials such as stone, wood, clay, iron, steel, copper and aluminium. Vessels made of clay are known as **earthenware**. Vessels used in ovens are made of glass and a special type of plastic. Baking trays are made of aluminium. Cooking vessels made of **ceramic** absorb heat. They stay hot even after cooking has finished. **Non-stick utensils** have a special coating on the surface that prevents food from sticking to the bottom of the utensil. Food in these utensils can be cooked with very less oil.

Non-stick pan

Clay vessel

Cooking Equipment

Different kinds of equipment are used for cooking. They are used to **generate** the heat required to cook the food. **Oven Toaster Grills** or OTGs, gas stoves, microwave ovens, tandoors, earthen *chulha* and solar cookers are some examples of cooking equipment.

Oven

Gas stove

Some cooking equipment such as microwaves, OTGs and tandoors provide dry heat. Earthen chulhas and gas stoves produce open flames.

generate: to produce or create something; **Oven Toaster Grills**: electric oven that can be used as a toaster and a grill

Cooking Fuels

LPG cylinder

Heat is produced by burning substances called **fuels**. Different kinds of fuels are used for cooking. Firewood, coal, charcoal and cow dung cakes are used in *chulhas* or *angithis*. These fuels are burnt and used by people living in small towns and villages. **Kerosene** is a liquid fuel used in kerosene stoves in different places of our country. **Liquefied Petroleum Gas (LPG)** is the most common fuel used in towns and cities. It is supplied in cylinders that are attached to the gas stoves with pipes. In many cities, LPG is supplied through pipelines.

Kettles, toasters, microwave ovens and many other cooking equipments use electricity as a fuel. The heat of the Sun produces **solar energy**. Solar cookers use this energy to cook food. However, food in solar cooker gets cooked slowly.

LPG, electricity and solar energy do not produce any smoke. Therefore, they are known as **clean fuels**. On the other hand, firewood, coal, charcoal, cow dung and kerosene produce smoke that **pollutes** the air.

Give it a shot

Make a list of some of the food items you love to eat and complete the following table.

Food items	Method of cooking	Cooking equipment	Fuel

Healthy Food

Food needs to be washed and cooked properly before eating. Washing cleans the food and cooking kills the germs present in it. Overcooking spoils the nutrients present in food. Food that is eaten raw should be washed carefully and eaten fresh.

Food that has low levels of nutrients is called **junk food**. Chips, ice cream, burgers and doughnuts are examples of junk food. Junk food is unhealthy. Fresh food cooked at home has plenty of nutrients that we need to be healthy.

Think through

Why is baked and roasted food healthier than fried food?

Junk food

pollute: to make the air dirty

Eating with Family

We eat three meals in a day—breakfast, lunch and dinner. We should always try to eat these meals on time. Eating with family is also important as it encourages togetherness. We should try to eat at least one meal of the day with our family members. Food is cooked at home for all the members of family. However, different kinds of food are cooked for people as per their age and nutrition requirements. Family members who are sick are given special food, which helps them get well quickly. Infants drink milk and are given special baby food. Young children eat plenty of fresh vegetables and fruits so that they grow healthy. Very old members of the family need soft and less spicy food that is easy to digest.

Eating with family

Wrap up

- Food can either be cooked or eaten raw.
- Cooking kills germs, makes food soft, tasty, easy to chew and digest.
- Boiling and steaming are some of the methods of cooking using water.
- Frying, baking, grilling and roasting are some of the methods of cooking without water.
- Different types of utensils and stoves are used for cooking.
- Fuels are materials that are used as a source of heat.
- It is important to eat clean, healthy and well-balanced food.
- Members of a family eat different kinds of food depending on their age and nutrition requirements.

Brush up

A Fill in the blanks with the correct answers.

1. .... can be eaten raw.

   a. Pulses   b. Ladies' finger   c. Cucumber   d. Rice

2. Dhokla is cooked by ....

   a. baking   b. grilling   c. steaming   d. frying

3. A cooking method which is unhealthy is ....

a. baking   b. steaming   c. frying   d. boiling

4. A fuel that does not pollute the air is ....

a. LPG   b. firewood   c. coal   d. wood

5. .... is known as a clean fuel.

a. Firewood   b. Coal   c. Solar energy   d. wood

B **Find the names of <u>six</u> methods of cooking, <u>three</u> items of food, <u>two</u> types of fuels and <u>one</u> cooking equipment from the word grid. One has been done for you.**

G	F	N	C	B	M	O	M	O	G
A	R	M	O	A	I	V	E	T	R
S	I	C	A	K	E	L	F	G	I
B	O	I	L	I	N	G	R	O	L
T	M	O	M	N	U	R	Y	V	L
I	D	L	I	G	N	I	I	E	I
K	R	O	A	S	T	I	N	G	N
S	T	E	A	M	I	N	G	A	G

C **Write T for true or F for false.**

1. Boiling is an unhealthy method of cooking. ☐
2. Grilling food needs a lot of oil. ☐
3. All family members should try to eat at least one meal together. ☐
4. All food needs to be cooked before eating. ☐
5. Food cannot be cooked without heat. ☐

D **Answer these questions.**

1. Why do we cook food before eating?
2. What are the different materials used for making cooking vessels?
3. Why should we eat together as a family?
4. What are cooking methods? Write about any three of them.
5. What is junk food? Why is it unhealthy?

Learn the ropes

Talk to some people in your neighbourhood and collect information about the types of fuels they use for cooking. Which fuels are less polluting and why? Discuss in class.

Put your heads together

In groups, make charts about topics related to food and cooking. Group A will work on 'healthy and unhealthy food', group B will work on 'cooking methods and vessels', and group C will work on 'fuels used for cooking and eating together in a family'. You can either write about each topic, make drawings about it or collect pictures about the topic. A volunteer from each group can present the chart in the classroom.

Cross connect

Bring ingredients from home to make a sandwich with the help of an elder.

Ingredients: Two slices of bread, butter, cheese slices, sliced cucumber, tomato, salt and pepper

1. Apply butter on one side of a slice of bread.
2. Place a slice of cheese on it.
3. Add cucumber and tomato slices. Sprinkle salt and pepper.
4. Place the other slice of bread on top and press it with your hand.

Your sandwich is ready!

11 Water in Our Lives

Get the ball rolling

What are the main sources of water in your locality? From where do you get water? Does it look clean enough for drinking?

All living things need water to live and grow. It is important for both plants and animals.

Water for Plants

Plants use water, sunlight and air to make their food. However, not all plants need the same amount of water. Some plants such as cacti, keekar and date palms can live on very little water. Tea, money plant and rice need a lot of water to grow. When plants do not get enough water, they **droop** or **wilt**.

Plants droop when they don't get enough water

Water for Animals

Animals need water to drink and bathe. Rattlesnakes and camels need less water. Camels can stay without water for long periods. Animals that live in cold regions need little water.

droop: to bend or hang; **wilt**: when a plant dries up

This is because they are inactive during winters and sleep for a long time. This is called **hibernation**. Animals that live in hot regions drink a lot of water. Some animals such as buffaloes and elephants **wade** in water to cool off their bodies.

Buffaloes wade in water to cool off

We get water from different sources. Let us learn more about them.

Sources of Water

Almost three-fourth of the Earth's surface is covered with water. Let us say if the Earth is divided into four parts, then one part of the Earth would be made of land; rest three parts would be made of water. Most of the water on the Earth is found in **seas** and **oceans**. They are the main sources of water on Earth. However, we cannot drink this water directly as it is salty. We drink water from **freshwater sources**.

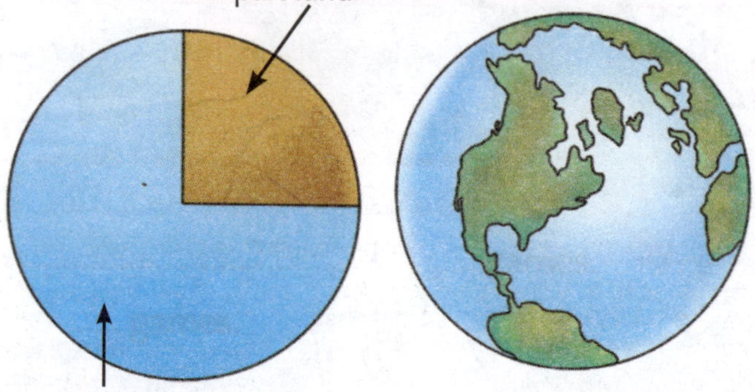

Most of the Earth's surface is covered with water

Freshwater

Rainwater is the only natural source of freshwater on Earth. It is the purest form of water. Rainwater collects in **rivers**, **streams**, **lakes** and **ponds**. It seeps into the soil as **groundwater**. It can be drawn by digging **wells**, or by using **tube wells** and **handpumps**. Farmers use tube wells to water their crops.

Clued in

The Pacific Ocean is the largest ocean in the world.

Well

Pond

Stream

River

hibernation: spending winter in a deep sleep; **wade**: to walk in not very deep water

Forms of Water

Water is found in three forms—ice (solid), water (liquid) and water vapour (gas).

Water changes into ice on cooling

Water changes into water vapour on heating

Water vapour changes back to water on cooling

Uses of Water

Some of the uses of water are:

- Water is used for drinking, washing, bathing, cleaning and cooking.
- Water is used for generating electricity.
- Water is important for digestion of food and removal of waste materials from our bodies.
- Farmers need water to grow crops.
- Water is used for water sports like swimming, rafting and surfing.
- Boats and ships move on rivers and seas.
- Rivers and water bodies are an important part of religious festivals. Boat races are held on Onam and religious rituals are carried out around a river during Chhath Puja.

Bathing

Rafting

Water We Get at Our Homes

Water reaches our homes from rivers and lakes. However, this water is not fit for drinking because it contains **impurities** and germs. Therefore, water is first sent to a **water treatment plant** for **purification**. Clean water is then collected in tanks and reaches our homes through pipelines. Clean water does not have any taste, colour or smell.

A water treatment plant

impurities: a substance that is present in small quantities in something and makes it impure; **purification**: the process of making something pure by removing harmful materials

Drinking Water

Water from taps carries a lot of germs which can make us sick. Water which is clean and fit for drinking is called **potable water**. Tap water should either be boiled or **filtered** at home to make it fit for drinking. We should always drink clean water.

Water filter

In some places, especially in villages, water available is not enough to meet the needs of all the people. Villagers sometimes have to travel long distances to **fetch** water from wells or handpumps. They often stand in queues to collect water from wells and taps. Sometimes, water is supplied to these villages by water tanks.

People in villages queue up to get water

Getting clean drinking water is the right of every human being. The local government should provide clean drinking water to all, be it in villages, towns or cities.

Give it a shot

1. Find the name of the river or any other water body from where you get water at your home.
2. Name some important lakes and rivers in your state. Collect pictures and paste them in your notebook.

Think through

When water that comes to your house has a colour or smell, what does it mean?

Why we wash our hands and feet before entering our homes

Houses provide us shelter and protection. Therefore, we should keep them clean. Shoes or sandals become dirty when we step outside our houses. We should remove them and wash our hands and feet before entering the house. In olden days, people would travel barefoot for long distances. If these places were dirty, germs would enter the house. So, it is necessary to clean up before entering the house.

filtered: to clean water by passing it through a sieve; **fetch**: to go and get something

Wrap up

- All living things need water to live and grow.
- The surface of the Earth is covered with salty water present in seas and oceans.
- We get water from different sources.
- Rainwater is a natural source of water. It is the purest form of water.
- Freshwater is found in rivers, lakes and ponds. It seeps into the soil as groundwater.
- Water from different waterbodies reaches our homes through pipelines.

Brush up

A Fill in the blanks with the correct answers.

1. Ice is a .... form of water.
   a. solid   b. liquid   c. gas   d. purest
2. Some plants like .... can live on little water.
   a. tea   b. keekar   c. rice   d. wheat
3. Water is important for ....
   a. non-living things   b. living things   c. stars   d. soil
4. Water from sea is not fit for drinking because it is ....
   a. dirty   b. salty   c. hot   d. cold

B Match the following.

1. Oceans	a. Without impurities
2. Clean water	b. Rainwater
3. Filtered water	c. Gas
4. Water vapour	d. Potable water
5. Freshwater	e. Salty

C Write T for true and F for false.

1. We should drink water from wells and taps. ☐
2. Water is important for all living things. ☐
3. The water from seas and oceans is fit for drinking. ☐

4. Germs in water are killed by boiling.

5. Water exists in three forms.

D Answer these questions.

1. Do all plants need equal amount of water?
2. What is groundwater? How can we use groundwater?
3. What is potable water?
4. What are the three forms of water?
5. What are some of the uses of water?
6. How does water reach our homes? How can we clean water and make it fit for drinking at home?
7. There are places where water is not easily available. How do the people in these places get water?

Learn the ropes

How will you ensure that drinking water is available to animals and birds during summers?

Put your heads together

In groups of four, make a list of activities you do with water every day. Based on this information, make a chart on how useful water is in your daily life.

Cross connect

1. Write a poem, or a song on water.
2. Make a list of the uses of water and draw pictures about them and colour them.

12 Storing and Saving Water

Get the ball rolling

How do you store water in your home? Have you seen water being wasted? How can we avoid it? Do you reuse water?

We have learnt that water from freshwater sources such as rivers, lakes, ponds and groundwater is used for drinking and cleaning. Underground water is obtained from wells, handpumps and tube wells. Water is found in solid form as ice or snow on the mountains. It is also found as liquid in rivers, seas and oceans, and as gas in the form of water vapour in the air around us.

Snow on mountains is a source of water

River is a source of freshwater

Water in Liquid Form

Water can be stored in containers of different shapes and sizes. Water in liquid form does not have a fixed shape or size. It takes the shape of the container in which it is kept. Water poured on a flat surface flows and spreads.

Water takes the shape of the container it is poured into

Let us do an activity to understand this.

Take a cup, a glass, a tray and a bottle full of water. Pour water from the bottle into them. What do you observe? Water takes the shape of the container it is poured into. This shows that water has no shape of its own.

Same volume of water takes different shapes in different containers

Now, take a tall bottle and a large wide-mouthed bowl. Using a tall measuring glass, pour the same amount of water in both containers. The containers have different shapes but the **volume** of the water is fixed. Volume is the space enclosed in a container. The bowl will be half-full because it has more space. The bottle will be almost full as it has less space. Different vessels or containers can hold different volumes of water. More volume of water can be stored in a large container.

A Rainy Day

A rainy day

Rain is the purest and the most important natural source of water on the Earth. Rain falls on the Earth in the form of **droplets**. It seeps under the ground as **groundwater**. Rain is important for both plants and animals. Plants look fresh and green when rain falls on them. Many insects and worms come out of the ground on rainy days because the ground is filled with water and it becomes difficult for them to breathe. Animals that live on the land try to find shelter as they fear **thunder**.

Clued in

A rain gauge is an instrument used to measure the amount of rainfall over a period of time.

droplets: a small drop of a liquid; **thunder**: a loud noise heard during rains

People enjoy rain as it brings down the temperature on a hot day. We all love feeling rainwater droplets on our palms. When the first droplets of rain fall on dry earth, we get a **unique** sweet smell. Children enjoy playing outdoors during rains. They make paper boats and sail them in rainwater.

Think through

Which bird dances when it rains?

Water Cycle

In nature, water changes into water vapour and then again into water. This process is known as the **water cycle**. During daytime, the Sun heats up the water in rivers and lakes, which slowly changes into water vapour and rises. The water vapour cools down and changes into tiny droplets that form **clouds**. As clouds become heavy, they cannot hold any more water droplets and fall on the Earth as rain. This process continues and water is circulated in nature.

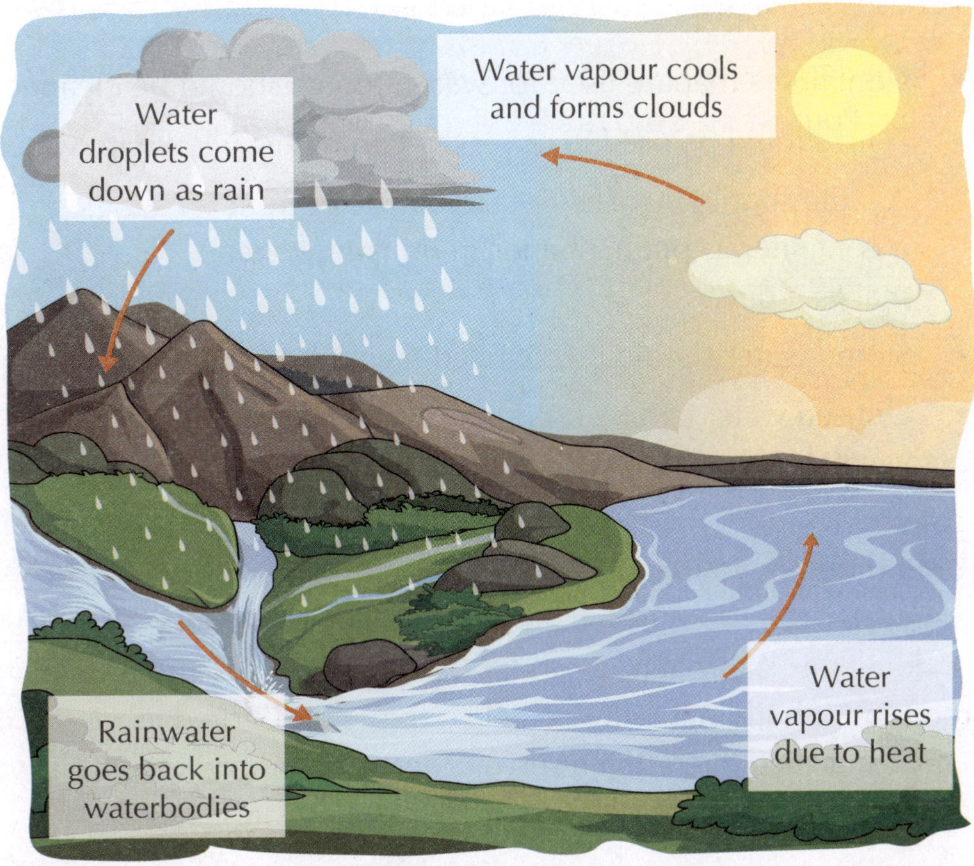

The water cycle

Storage of Water

Water is stored in different types of containers. These containers are made of different materials. People store water in **earthenware** made of clay, **ceramic** and stone. These pots are called *surahis*, *matkas* or *ghadas*.

Plastic containers

Matka

Containers made of steel, aluminium, copper and plastics are also used for storing water. These pots are called *surahis* and *ghadas*. Sometimes even buckets and drums are used for storing water.

unique: very special; **earthenware**: vessels or pots made up of baked clay; **ceramic**: a substance made of clay hardened by heat

In cities, people use underground as well as overhead tanks to store water. The main water supply is connected to these tanks through pipelines. It is important that water stored in different containers or tanks be kept clean. Drinking water should be stored carefully so that water does not become unfit for drinking.

Water storage tanks

The steps that can be taken to ensure that drinking water stays clean are:

- Containers that are used for water storage should be cleaned regularly.
- A lid should be used to cover the containers filled with water.
- A ladle should be used to take out water from a container as putting hands in drinking water makes it dirty.
- Stored water should be changed regularly.
- Unused water can be used to wash clothes, clean vegetables and in mopping the floor.

Give it a shot

Find out which containers are used to store water at homes. Draw or paste pictures of these containers in your notebook.

Rainwater Harvesting

Collecting rainwater

Rainwater can be collected and reused later. One of the simplest methods of doing this is through **rainwater harvesting**. Rainwater is collected from rooftops of buildings with the help of pipes and stored in **reservoirs** or **tanks**. It is then filtered in reservoirs and sent to **borewells**. This water can be used for watering plants in gardens and irrigating fields.

Shortage of Water

6 CLEAN WATER AND SANITATION

An increase in the **population** can cause an imbalance in nature. Sometimes, the amount of water present is not enough for all people. This is called shortage of water. It is caused due to several reasons. Many lakes and rivers dry up in summer because of heat. They are **replenished** by rainfall. However, if the rainfall received is low, these water bodies are not

An increase in the population can cause shortage of water

Clued in

Dehydration is an excessive loss of water from the body leading to headache, dizziness and dryness.

population: all the people who live in a particular area; **replenished**: to make something full again refilled. In summers, the groundwater level becomes low. Therefore, taking out water from wells, tubewells and hand pumps also becomes difficult.

Reasons for shortage of water

Some of the reasons of water shortage are:

- Trees increase rainfall and cutting them down reduces the amount of freshwater on the Earth.

- An increase in the population has led to overuse of water.
- Wastage of water in different activities such as washing and cleaning causes shortage of water.
- Water from rivers and lakes is being used up very fast, but is not getting refilled.

Ways of saving water

We should save water and use it wisely. Some of the ways to save water are:

- Do not keep taps running while brushing teeth.

- Use a bucket of water and a mug to take a bath instead of using a shower.
- Use water that is left behind after washing clothes for cleaning terraces, balconies or cars.

- Use a watering can to water plants in a garden.
- Use a bucket and a **sponge** to wash cars instead of a **hosepipe**.
- Wash vegetables in a bowl instead of washing them under a tap.
- Check taps, pipes and toilets for leaks.
- Practise rainwater harvesting to collect and save water at homes, schools and other places in the neighbourhood.
- Do not dump waste materials from houses and factories in the water bodies.

Wrap up

* Rainwater is the purest form of water.
* Oceans, seas, rivers, streams, lakes and ponds are the water bodies found on the surface of the Earth.

sponge: a piece of soft, light and absorbent material used for cleaning; **hosepipe**: a long tube of rubber or plastic used to direct water onto something

- Water in the form of liquid does not have any fixed shape or size. It takes the shape of the vessel it is poured into.
- In nature, water changes into water vapour and then again into water. This is known as the water cycle.
- Water is stored in containers made up of different materials.
- Rainwater harvesting is a method of storing and reusing rainwater.
- Drinking water should be stored in clean containers.

Brush up

A Unscramble the names of these water bodies.

1. ENOCA ....
2. VERIR ....
3. ASE ....
4. KAEL ....
5. DOPN ....

B Fill in the blanks with the correct answers.

1. .... (Rainwater/Groundwater) is collected from rooftops of buildings with the help of pipes.
2. The containers have .... (same/different) shapes but the volume of water is fixed.
3. Trees increase rainfall and cutting them down .... (increases/reduces) the amount of freshwater on the Earth.
4. .... (Less/More) volume of water can be stored in a large container.
5. Rainwater .... (irrigation/harvesting) should be practised to collect and save water.

C Write T for true and F for false.

1. Water in liquid form has fixed shape and size. ☐
2. Volume refers to the space of the container. ☐
3. Rain replenishes only underground water. ☐
4. Watering plants with watering can saves water. ☐
5. Water vapour is formed at night when the temperature cools down. ☐

D Answer these questions.

1. What do you understand by volume?
2. What is water cycle?
3. Why is rain important?
4. Why do we store water?
5. What is rainwater harvesting?
6. What are the reasons of shortage of water?
7. What are the ways of saving water?

Learn the ropes

'Save water, save life.' Discuss this in class and note down the important points. Make a poster for saving water.

Put your heads together

In groups, find out how much water is stored every day at your homes? How much water is used for drinking or bathing and how much water is wasted?

Make a list of things you can do at home to stop wastage of water. Share it with the other groups.

Cross connect

Describe and draw a scene from a rainy day with details about birds, animals, plants and yourself.

13 Our Houses

Get the ball rolling

Have you seen houses like the ones shown in these pictures? Where do you find them? What kind of a house do you live in?

A house is a place where we live with our family. It gives us shelter from heat, cold and rain as well as protects us from animals and thieves. Early humans did not know how to build houses. They lived in caves and on trees. Later they learnt how to build houses using materials easily available near them.

Types of Houses

Houses are of different types. This maybe because of the **material** used for building the houses and the **location** where they are built. Houses can also be **temporary** or **permanent**.

Kutcha houses

Houses made of mud, straw, leaves and bamboo are called **kutcha houses**. A **hut** is an example of a kutcha house. The roofs of kutcha houses are made of dried straw, palm leaves

temporary: something that lasts only for a limited time

or tin sheets. These are called **thatched roofs**. Some kutcha houses have sloping roofs. Kutcha houses are mostly found in villages. They can easily get destroyed in heavy rains and storms.

People building a kutcha house

Pucca houses

Human beings learnt about new and improved methods of building houses. They started building houses using materials such as bricks, cement, iron, steel and stone. These stronger houses are called **pucca houses**. They do not get easily destroyed by strong winds and heavy rains. Bungalows, double-storeyed houses and multi-storeyed buildings, which have many apartments or flats in them, are examples of pucca houses. They are mostly found in towns and big cities. Pucca houses are more expensive. They are **permanent** houses as they cannot be moved.

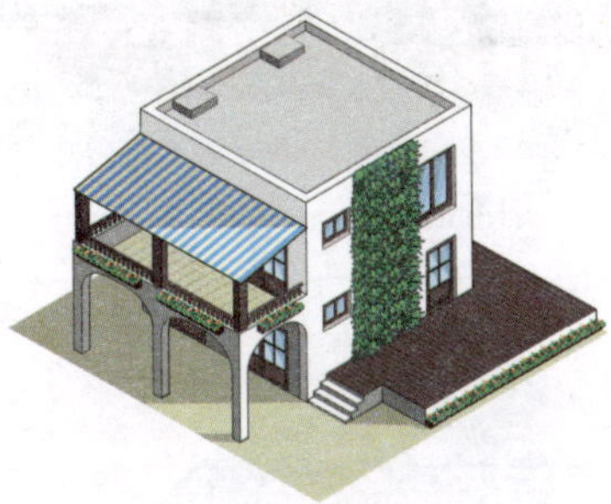

Pucca house

Bungalow

Multi-storeyed apartments

Uncommon Houses

Houses are also built according to the region and climate of the place. We find different kinds of houses in different parts of India and in other countries. These houses are special and are found only in those particular regions.

Houses built in hill stations of India have sloping roofs so that rainwater and snow slide easily to the ground. These houses are made of wood because it is easily available from the trees growing in the forests in the hills and mountains. Kashmir, Sikkim and Manali have such houses.

House with sloping roof

permanent: a thing that lasts for a long time

Stilt houses

Look at the picture. Why do you think this house is standing on legs? These legs are structures called **stilts** and the houses built on stilts are called **stilt houses**. In regions that receive heavy rainfall, houses are often raised on stilts because of the danger of **floods**. To protect the houses from flood water, snakes and water insects, they are built above the ground. Stilt houses are found in the northeastern states of India. They are also called **pile dwellings**.

Stilt house

Houseboats

Houseboats or **floating houses** are boats that have been designed or modified to be used as houses. They are found in Kashmir and Kerala. Not all houseboats move across lakes because not all of them are fitted with motors. These houseboats remain **anchored** to the land.

Houseboat

Igloos

Houses built in very cold regions like the Arctic are made from slabs of compressed snow which is **abundantly** available. Such houses are called **igloos**. Although igloos are made of ice, they remain warm because of the air pockets present in the blocks of ice. The single opening in an igloo also helps to conserve warmth. Igloos protect the people living in cold countries like Greenland from icy cold winds.

Igloo

Log cabins

Log cabins are houses made of logs of wood. These logs are kept horizontally, one on top of the other. Spaces between the logs are filled with mud and chips of wood. These buildings are small structures found in the forests or woods. The forest officers and rangers use log huts. Nowadays, a few resorts also offer log huts for the guests.

Log cabin

stilts: wooden or metal sticks that keep a house above the ground; **floods:** when water from a water body overflows and spills to nearby areas; **anchored**: a heavy object attached to a boat with a rope that keeps it from moving away on water; **abundantly:** existing in large quantities; more than enough

Tepees

Tepees are cone-shaped tents made with sticks and animal skins. They are popular among people who go **camping** or **trekking**. The first tents or tepees were used by the native Americans. They were made out of the skin of buffaloes. Nowadays, tents are made of waterproof material like nylon or polyester.

Tepee

Caravan

A **caravan** is a house on wheels. It is also known as a **travel trailer**. In the olden days, caravans were pulled by horses, cows or bullocks. They provided a safe place to sleep and were more comfortable than a tent. Nowadays, caravans are attached to cars and trucks. Modern caravans are called **recreation vehicles** or **RVs**. They have bathrooms, shower units, kitchen and sleeping areas. It is a home on wheels.

Caravan

Caravans, tepees and tents are houses that can be moved from place to place. Therefore, they are temporary houses.

Neat and Clean

Wherever we live and whatever type of house we live in, it is very important that we keep our house and our neighbourhood clean. It is not possible for only our parents or any one person in the house to keep it clean all the time. It is the responsibility of each member of the house to do their part in keeping their house neat and clean. On weekends, our parents often ask us to tidy our rooms, put away our books, toys and clothes in their appropriate places.

Think through

Why is it important to keep the area around the house clean?

To keep the house clean, we must remember these points:

- Doors and windows in a house should be kept open to let in fresh air and sunlight. Sunlight kills germs in the air inside the house.
- The windows in a house should have a wire mesh to keep flies and the mosquitoes out.

camping: living in a tent; **trekking**: going on a long, difficult journey on foot

- Houses should be swept, dusted and mopped daily. A **disinfectant** should be added to the mop water.
- Bathrooms and toilets should be cleaned daily and kept dry.
- Cobwebs should be removed regularly.
- Things should be kept in their proper places. A house neatly arranged looks clean.
- Garbage should be thrown in dustbins with a lid.
- Food, water or milk that spills on the floor should be cleaned immediately.
- Garbage should not be allowed to collect outside the houses as these are **breeding places** for germs and mosquitoes that cause many diseases.

Throw garbage in the bin

Give it a shot

What is the difference between a house and a home? We all love our homes and we like to see our homes always clean. Circle the things in the image that are not kept in their proper place.

Decorating the House

Birthday parties, marriages, anniversaries and festivals are special occasions when we like to decorate our houses. We also wear new and special clothes. Balloons, **streamers**, lights and **rangolis** are some of the ways we decorate our homes depending on the occasion. Flowers, coloured powered rice or powder colours are used to make **rangolis**. Rangolis are beautiful designs made on the floor of the house at the entrance or just

Rangoli

Clued in

Warli art is a type of painting done on the walls of the houses. It was made by women on special occasions using rice paste on red coloured mud walls of huts. Bamboo sticks were used as a paintbrush.

disinfectant: a cleaning liquid that kills germs; **breeding places**: dirty places where germs and mosquitoes live; **streamers**: long and colourful materials made using soft paper, used for decoration outside the entrance. This is very popular in West Bengal and South India. People fond of gardening have lots of plants in their homes. Potted plants kept inside the house also decorate our houses. People also decorate the walls of their house by painting them and using mirror work. Wall paintings are very popular in Bihar, Gujarat, Maharashtra and West Bengal.

Think through

Why do you think people make rangolis in front of their uses on special occasions?

Wrap up

- A house provides shelter and protects us from wild animals and thieves.
- Houses are made from materials that are easily available.
- Kutcha houses are made using materials like mud, straw, leaves and bamboo.
- Pucca houses are made using materials like bricks, cement, iron and steel.
- Some uncommon houses are built according to the region and climate of the area.
- Houses that cannot be moved are permanent houses.
- Houses that can be moved from one place to another are temporary houses.
- It is important to keep our houses clean. Every member of the family should be responsible in keeping the house clean.
- We decorate our homes in different ways during special occasions and festivals.

Brush up

A Fill in the blanks.

1. Houses are built keeping the .... of a place in mind.
2. It is the duty of .... to keep the house neat and clean.
3. A .... house can be easily destroyed by strong winds and heavy rainfall.
4. In places where it rains heavily people make houses on ....
5. Windows should be opened to let in .... so that the germs are killed.

B Fill in the blanks with the correct answers.

1. .... determines the type of houses built in a region.

   a. Climate b. Scenery c. People d. Water

2. Igloos are found in ....
   a. India   b. Greenland   c. Nepal   d. Sri Lanka
3. The first kind of tents used were called ....
   a. tepee   b. travel trailers
   c. igloos   d. caravans
4. .... is a building that has many apartments and flats.
   a. Multi-storeyed building   b. Bungalows
   c. Igloos   d. Double-storeyed building
5. Rangoli is very popular in ....
   a. Punjab   b. Haryana   c. Kerala   d. West Bengal

C Match the following.

1.	A home on a vehicle pulled by a car or truck	a.	Log cabin
2.	A house made of ice and snow	b.	Tepee
3.	Houses built on stilts	c.	Igloo
4.	A small house built with logs of wood	d.	Pile dwellings
5.	Floating houses on lakes	e.	Caravan
6.	A house made with sticks and animal skin	f.	Houseboats

D Answer these questions.

1. Why does everyone need a house?
2. Why do we need windows in a house?
3. List any four ways in which we can keep our houses clean.
4. What kinds of houses are found in Manali and Kashmir?
5. How are kutcha houses different from pucca houses?

Learn the ropes

While on a school trip to a historical monument, what would you do in the following situations? Write Y for yes and N for no.

- Run around and touch the things on display. ☐
- Enjoy eating chips with friends and throw the packet in a corner. ☐
- Proudly write your name on the wall. ☐
- Walk in a line and follow the teacher's instructions. ☐
- Listen carefully to announcements. ☐

Put your heads together

In groups, write down a charter on cleanliness for your class. Each group will present their points and then discuss them together as a class. Come up with one common charter for your class.

Cross connect

Make a log cabin using wooden ice cream sticks. You will need white glue, used ice cream sticks, cardboards and a pair of scissors. Use glue to keep the ice cream sticks together. Paste the log cabin on a cardboard and display it in class.

14 Animals in Our Homes

Get the ball rolling

Do you have a pet? Which animal lives with you? Where in your house do these animals live? Which of them are seen only at night?

We keep **pet animals** for company, protection or **entertainment**. We should treat them with kindness and give them enough attention, care and love. Pets are also wonderful friends. Dogs, cats and rabbits are some common pet animals.

Domestic Animals

A goat is a domestic animal

Domestic animals are tamed by human beings so that they live and breed under their care and work for them. They depend on human beings for food, shelter and water. We keep domestic animals on farms or at our homes. Cow, goat, horse, sheep, hen and camel are some domestic animals.

entertainment: activities that provide enjoyment to people

Domestic animals provide us many useful things. Hens give us eggs, cows and goats give us milk, sheep give us wool, horses and camels carry loads. Buffaloes give us milk and help us draw carts and plough fields.

Food for pet and domestic animals

Pets and domestic animals need healthy and clean food. They should be fed at regular intervals. Different animals need different kinds of food. Dogs eat milk, egg, meat, bread and biscuits. Meat, fish, milk and bread are given to cats. Cows and buffaloes eat grass. Parrots and hens feed grains and seeds.

Cow eats grass

Cat drinks milk

Dog eats biscuits

Hen eats seeds

Shelter for pet and domestic animals

Pets and domestic animals need shelter to protect themselves from sunlight, heat, strong winds, rain and cold. They also need shelters to raise their young ones. Clean and comfortable shelters must be given to the animals that live with us. Animal shelters must be cleaned regularly.

Clued in

A group of kittens is called a kindle and a group of cats is called a clowder.

Cows are kept in sheds

Hens are kept in coops

Horses are kept in stables

Unwanted Animals in Our Houses

There are some animals which enter our houses quietly when we are not around and eat our food. These are **unwanted animals**. They spoil our things and sometimes even cause diseases. Cockroaches, lizards, mosquitoes, rats, spiders, flies and ants are examples of harmful animals. They are also known as **pests**. Most pests live in drains, dark corners of the kitchen, in gaps of cabinets

Mouse

Lizard

Cockroach

Housefly

and in warm, moist places. Rats, houseflies and mosquitoes are active both during day and night. Rats and mice enter our houses and nibble on food. If sweet food is left open, ants gather around it and start feeding on it. Sometimes, we even see houseflies flying over our food. Cockroaches come out at night in search of food. Some pests like lizards help us by eating insects. Food tasted or touched by any animal should never be eaten as it is bad for our health.

Give it a shot

Write the names of some pets you know of. Name some pet and domestic animals other than those given in the chapter. How can you take care of them? Draw their pictures in your notebook.

Getting rid of pests

Some of the ways of getting rid of pests are:

- We should clean dishes right after we finish eating and throw leftovers in a closed dustbin. We should clean the kitchen by removing any **crumbs** or spills.
- Food should always be kept covered. Uncovered food attracts flies and mosquitoes.

Think through

What should you know before you bring a puppy, a kitten or any other animal home? Whom should you talk to?

- Houses should be swept and mopped with a disinfectant every day.
- **Pesticides** should be sprayed in sewers and drains, and water should not be allowed to collect in puddles. This will prevent mosquitoes from **breeding**.
- We should try to keep the surroundings of our houses clean by never dumping garbage in the open. It attracts houseflies and causes diseases.
- We should use wire mesh on doors and windows to prevent insects from entering the house.

Animal Care

Pet animals need proper care so that they stay healthy and fit. When animals are sick or injured, they are taken to special hospitals for animals. A doctor who treats them is known as a veterinary doctor or a vet. If an animal falls sick, we should take them to a vet immediately.

Veterinary doctor

crumb: tiny pieces that fall from bread, biscuits or cake; **pesticides:** a chemical used for killing pests, especially insects; **breeding:** the producing of young animals and plants

Kindness towards animals

Many animals in our society are suffering. They are **abused** or **neglected**. Some go hungry on streets. Many suffer at the hands of their owners, who either don't understand or don't care about the animals.

Animals are a wonderful part of our lives. They bring us joy and make us laugh. They give us unconditional love. We can take care of animals in the following ways:

- We should feed stray animals in our locality regularly and ask adults to get them **vaccinated**.
- We should report animal abuse or cruelty to the concerned authorities.
- We should take care of our pets and treat them like family.
- We should encourage others to be kind towards animals.
- We should try to adopt animals and not buy them.

We should be kind to animals

Wrap up

- We keep pet animals for company, protection or entertainment.
- Pet animals and domestic animals depend on us for food, shelter and protection.
- Domestic animals are tamed by humans to live and breed under their care and to work for them.
- Animals who enter our house on their own in search of food are called unwanted animals.
- Unwanted animals can be stopped from entering the house by keeping the house and surroundings clean.
- Animals who are injured or are sick are taken to special hospitals for animals where veterinary doctors or vets treat them.

abused: to treat someone with cruelty; **neglected:** when someone does not receive proper treatment or care; **vaccinated:** inject vaccine to prevent infection

Brush up

A Fill in the blanks.

1. Animals that have been tamed by humans to live and breed under their care are called ....
2. Animals which enter our houses on their own in search of food are called ....
3. .... animals are kept mainly for a person's company, protection, or entertainment.
4. The doctor who treats animals is known as ....

B Look at the pictures and write Domestic Animal or Pet Animal under each.

1. ....

2. ....

3. ....

4. ....

5. ....

6. ....

7. ....

8. ....

C Fill in the blanks with the correct answers.

1. If .... food is left open, ants gather around it and start feeding on it.
   a. sweet b. salty c. spoilt
2. The doctor who treats animals is known as a ....
   a. paediatrician b. vet c. physician
3. We should .... animals.
   a. buy b. borrow c. adopt
4. We keep .... animals for company and protection.
   a. wild b. pet c. domestic
5. Animals who enter our house on their own in search of food are called .... animals.
   a. unwanted b. domestic c. stray

D Answer these questions.

1. What are domestic animals?
2. What are pet animals?
3. Why do animals need shelter?
4. Name some useful things that we get from domestic animals.
5. Write four ways in which we can get rid of unwanted animals.
6. How can we take care of animals?

Learn the ropes

1. Visit an animal hospital or a veterinary doctor's clinic. Find out:
   a. ways in which we can take care of pet and domestic animals in different seasons
   b. what they should eat, and c. what they should not eat.
   Present your observations in the form a chart in class.
2. If you found a lost pet, how would you help it reach its owner?

Put your heads together

Cut out pictures or draw the pictures of five domestic animals. Write their names, shelters and the names of their young ones.

Cross connect

Make a list of three pests present in your home. Write what are they called in your mother tongue. Draw or paste their pictures.

Pest	Name in mother tongue	Picture

15 Mapping Places

Get the ball rolling

Have you seen a map of your neighbourhood? Can you find your way home from where your school bus drops you? In case your school friend wants to come to your house, can you give him or her directions?

Map

A **map** is a drawing of a particular area such as a neighbourhood, city, country or continent, on a flat surface like paper. Maps show the shape and position of different countries and their borders. They also show natural features such as rivers and mountains. Features like roads and buildings are also shown on some maps. A collection or a book of maps is called an **atlas**.

Atlas

Map

Map scale

Maps are always drawn using the real measurements of a place. Of course, they cannot be as big as the area they represent. They are much smaller than the actual size of the place. Maps are drawn to **scale**, which means that they are drawn such that the actual size of an area can be measured. A scale also tells us about the distance between two points on a map. If the scale of a map is 1 cm=1 km, it means that 1 cm on the map represents 1 km on ground. Therefore, if the distance between two cities on this map is 10 cm, then the distance between them on ground will be 10 km.

Clued in

A person who makes maps is called a cartographer. The first maps were made by hand by painting them on paper. Most of the modern maps are made with the help of computers.

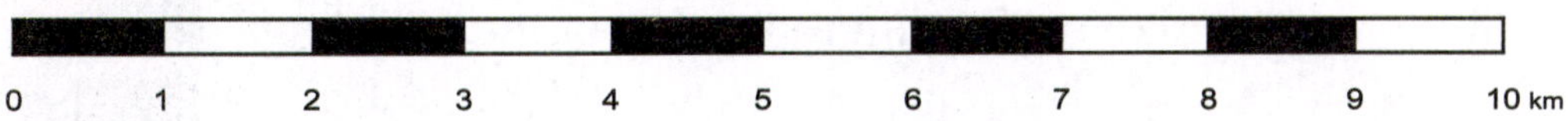

Map scale

Map symbols

Symbols are used on maps to show different places or features of a region. Symbols are small pictures that stand for different features on a map. They are often drawn to look like what they represent. For instance, a triangular shape is often used to **denote** a mountain on maps.

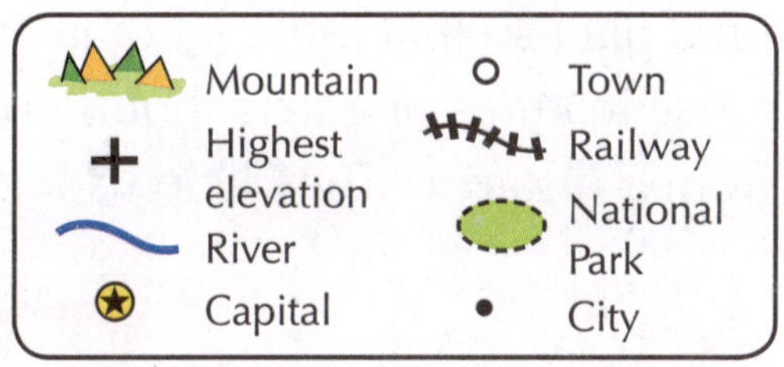

Map symbols

A **key**, or a **legend**, of a map tells us the meaning of the symbols used on a map. They are used to understand the symbols used on a map.

Colours are used to represent different kinds of landforms on a map. Forests are shown in green colour. Water bodies like rivers, seas and oceans are coloured blue and brown is used for mountains.

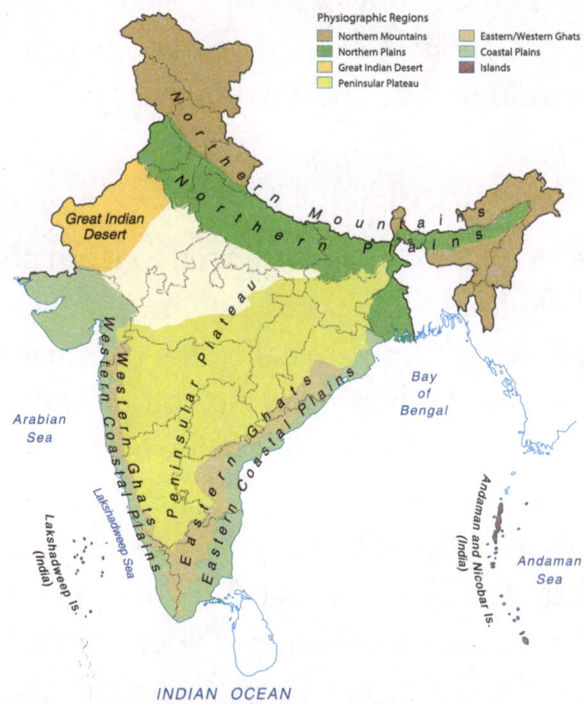

Colours are used to represent landforms

Globe

A globe is a model of the Earth. The word 'globe' means a **spherical** object. Therefore, globes are made spherical to look like the Earth. Continents and oceans are shown on a globe as they are on the Earth. However, because of its round shape

denote: to be a sign of something; **spherical**: round

we must keep turning the globe to see all the continents and oceans. Just like a map, a globe is also made to a scale. The difference is that a globe is difficult to carry as it is round and takes more space, while a map is flat and made on paper. So, it is easy to carry while travelling. Maps may not show the shape of the Earth but they show more details than a globe.

Globe

Plan

Drawings that show details of buildings such as a school or a house are called **plans**. **Architects** make plans of buildings or houses before they are built. Plans include details like the design of the rooms and other parts of the building. Like maps, plans are also made to a scale so that we get an idea of the size of the different parts of the building.

Plans are also made for cities, towns and even neighbourhoods. The plan of a neighbourhood shows where the houses, post offices, parks, schools and hospitals will be built. Symbols and signs are used on a plan so that these landmarks can be recognized. **Landmarks** are those features of a neighbourhood or a city that are easily recognized from a distance. They help us find the places located near them.

Plan of a house

Sketch

A rough drawing of a place is called a **sketch**. It shows the important landmarks of a place. These landmarks could be a hospital, a school or a park. Landmarks help us know where we are and find our **destination** easily.

> **Think through**
> Name any one landmark near your school and one near your home.

Directions

To draw a map, we first need to learn about directions. There are four **main directions**. They are **north**, **south**, **east** and **west**. These are called the **cardinal directions**. The top of a map is the north and the bottom is the south. On the right of the map, is east and on the left is west. In addition to the four main directions, there are other directions that are called **sub-directions**. These are **northeast**, **northwest**, **southeast** and **southwest**. The sub-directions lie between the cardinal directions. For example, if your school lies in between the north and the east, you will say that your school lies in the northeast.

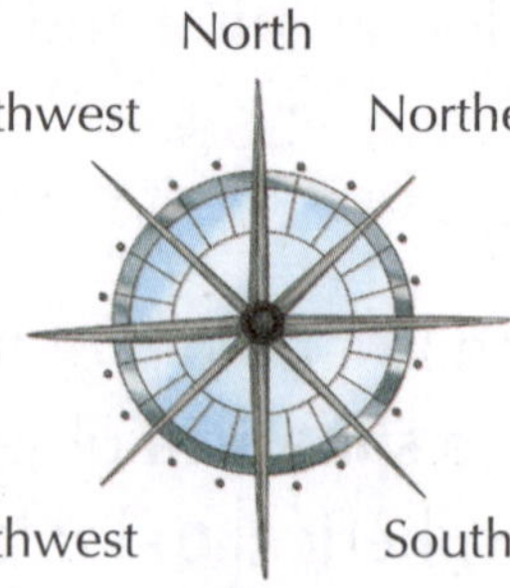

Cardinal and sub-directions

architect: a person who designs a building; **destination**: a place to which somebody is going or is being sent

Give it a shot

Amrit is a new student studying in Class 3 sitting in the front row. Amrit's teacher is standing to the east. Can you help Amrit find the directions and the things lying in those directions.

1. How many windows are there in the class? In which direction are the windows?
2. There is a fish tank in the class. In which direction is it?
3. Mention what lies to the north of Amrit.
4. In which direction should Amrit look to find out the time. What is the time on the class clock?
5. What is to the south of Amrit?

Compass

A **compass** is an instrument that shows directions. It has a needle that always points to the north. It helps us know the other three directions. In the olden days, before the compass was invented, travellers would use the movement of the Sun to help them know the time of day and the direction in which they were travelling. During night, the **Pole Star** would guide the traveller in the right direction. Nowadays, maps and compasses have been replaced by a technology called **GPS**. GPS stands for Global Positioning System. We use it to find our way when we are driving or walking.

Compass

Pole Star: a bright star that appears in the north of the sky

Maps are useful

Some of the uses of maps are:

- Maps are used to find directions while travelling to new cities and countries.
- Maps help us locate different places within a city or a neighbourhood that we would like to visit.
- Pilots and sailors find their position and location in the air or on the ocean with the help of maps.

Wrap up

- A map is a drawing of an area on a flat surface like paper.
- An atlas is a collection or a book of maps.
- Different colours are used on a map to show different features of a place or a country.
- Symbols are used to show different features on a map. A legend or a key tells us what these symbols mean.
- We first need to know the directions to draw a map.
- A drawing that shows the details of a building is called a plan.
- A sketch is a rough drawing of a place.
- The four main directions are north, south, east and west.
- A compass is an instrument that shows directions.
- Nowadays, both the map and the compass have been replaced by GPS.

Brush up

A Ashish's aunt and uncle came to visit him. Help Ashish explain to them the location of the places in his neighbourhood.

1. What lies to the North of Ashish's house?
2. What lies to the right of Ashish's house?
3. What is behind Ashish's house?
4. Where would Ashish reach if he turned left and then turned left again from his house?
5. What all would Ashish have to pass if he went to the temple?
6. What lies in between the school and the market?

B Write T for true and F for false.

1. In olden days, maps were made on paper by hand.
2. Different symbols are used on maps to show different features.
3. A legend shows the distance between two places on a map and their actual distance on ground.
4. A compass needle always points to the south.
5. A globe is a model of the Earth.

C Name them.

1. The bottom of this always has south ....
2. An instrument that has a needle to show directions ....
3. A small picture that stands for a particular feature on a map ....
4. This on a map tells us the distance between two places in reality ....
5. This is made by an architect ....

D Answer these questions.

1. What is a map?
2. What is a legend? What is it used for?

3. What is a compass? In which direction does its needle point?
4. What is the difference between a plan and a map?
5. What are the differences between a globe and a map?

Learn the ropes

Draw a map that explains the route from your house to a park in your neighbourhood.

Put your heads together

Make bookmarks using maps. You will need chart papers, maps of places you visited recently, scissors, ribbons or a string. Work in groups. Cut the chart papers into rectangles, roughly the size of bookmarks. Paste the map of the place you visited last on it. Punch a small hole on the top end and pass a ribbon or a string through it and tie it. Your bookmark is ready to remind you of the places you visited. You could make one for every new place you visit.

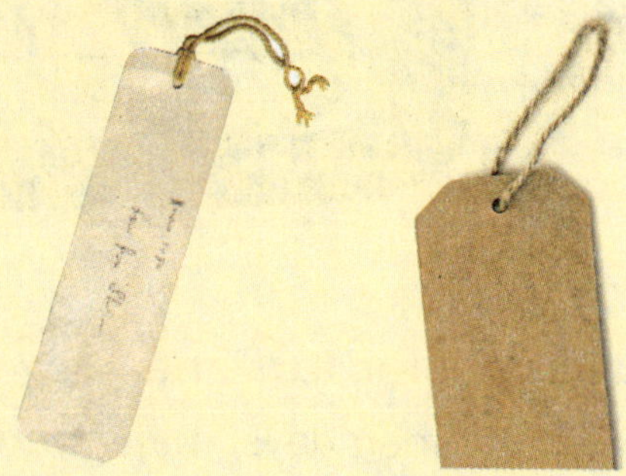

Cross connect

What are the landmarks that you see on your way to school? Do you see these on your way back from the school as well? Count and make a list of these landmarks.

16 Ways of Travelling

Get the ball rolling

Have you seen a bullock cart? What are the different kinds of vehicles that you have seen?

We see people on the roads in different vehicles when we go out. Do you sometimes wonder where so many people are going? People travel from one place to another for many reasons. Some people go to work and children go to school. People travel to the markets to deliver or buy daily supplies like milk, eggs and vegetables. During holidays, families travel to different places or sometimes to other countries. People go to the malls to watch films and to restaurants to eat delicious food. They also go out to meet their friends and relatives. People also travel to attend a wedding or a party.

Different types of vehicles

Vehicles are the means of transport that help move people and goods from one place to another. We see many kinds of vehicles on the roads. Some move slowly, while others can move very fast. Some vehicles move on land, some on water and some in the air. Can you name some of these vehicles?

Slow vehicle

Fast vehicle

History of Transport

Early humans travelled from one place to another by walking, running, or swimming. Then they learned to train animals such as donkeys, horses and camels to ride to places. These animals also helped them transport heavy loads from one place to another. The **wheel** was one of the most important **inventions** made by human beings. Using wheels, they invented carts that were pulled by animals. Bicycles, scooters, cars and trains were all invented over the years. All of them use the wheel.

Animal cart

Early humans made boats from tree trunks to help them travel across rivers and lakes. Then came the ships that could carry people across seas and oceans but they needed many people to **row** them. The invention of the **steam engine** and its use in trains and ships completely changed the manner of transportation as people were not dependent on animals for travel.

Boat made of a tree trunk

Transport on Land

All vehicles that move on land are means of **land transport**. These are carts, rickshaws, bicycles, scooters, motorcycles, cars, trucks, buses, trams, metro and trains. Land transport is the most common way of travelling. It is not expensive and is widely connected all over our country. In some villages, carts are still used to transport people and goods. Tractors are also used as a means of transport in villages.

Truck

Auto rickshaw

Cycle rickshaw

invention: a thing that has been made for the first time; **row**: moving a boat

Train travel

Train

Trains are used for travelling to far off cities in different parts of the country. Trams move within a city. Trains, metros and trams move on specially made metal tracks. Trains are a fast means of transport. Delhi, Kolkata, Chennai, Kochi, Lucknow, Mumbai, Hyderabad, Bengaluru and Jaipur have metros, which are a fast and convenient way of going to work within the cities, or even to places in nearby cities. Hundreds of people travel in a metro every day. In Mumbai, the local trains are popular with the working people.

We travel to hilly areas by the local trains of these regions. These are called the **Mountain Railways of India**. They were started more than a hundred years ago and are still working. Have you gone with your family on a train to Shimla or Darjeeling? If you do, you must travel on these trains.

Clued in

The first tram network was introduced in India in 1873 in Kolkata. These were horse-drawn trams. It is the only operational trams network in India and the oldest operating electric trams in Asia.

India has the world's fourth-largest railway network. Even small cities and towns in India have railway stations. People board trains at a railway station from allotted platforms. Trains carry both people and goods. Trains that carry only people are called **passenger trains**. Trains that carry only goods such as coal, wheat and rice are called **goods trains**.

Railway platform

A railway station is one of the busiest parts of a railway network. People are seen doing different jobs on a railway platform. When we enter a railway station, we see **porters** or **coolies** ready to carry our heavy luggage to help us place them in train carriages. On the platform, there are many stalls selling books, magazines, cold drinks and water. Some **vendors** sell tea and snacks. Inside the train, the **Travelling Ticket Examiner** (TTE) checks our tickets. There is an engine driver who drives the train. We also see guards carrying red or green flags. It is only when the guard raises the green flag and blows a whistle, that the train driver starts the train.

Transport on Water

All vehicles that sail on water are means of **water transport**. This is the oldest means of transport. Boats, ships, yachts, steamers and rafts are some of the vehicles used for water

vendors: a person who sells small things such as fruits, vegetables and newspapers transport. A ship is used for transporting large quantities of goods to far-off places. Fishermen too use boats to catch fish, which they then sell in the market. India's **coastline** is protected by the Indian Navy in their huge modern ships that stay on the sea. Many people go for a **cruise** on large modern ships called **liners**. **Ferries** carry passengers across rivers or lakes. **Submarines** are ships that move completely under water. These are used by the military and scientists.

Liner

Yacht

Raft

Transport by Air

All vehicles that move in the air are means of **air transport**. They carry both people and goods. Air transport is the fastest and the most modern means of transport. Aeroplanes, helicopters, hot air balloons, gliders and rockets are some of the means of air transport. People can travel from one city to another or to any part of the world in aeroplanes. People board them at airports from where they take off and land. Goods transported by aeroplanes also reach the airport from where they are loaded on a plane.

Aeroplane

Give it a shot

Tick (✓) the people or things that you see at an airport.

1. ☐ 2. ☐ 3. ☐ 4. ☐ 5. ☐

6. ☐ 7. ☐ 8. ☐ 9. ☐ 10. ☐

coastline: land along the coast; **cruise**: a journey by sea; **liner**: a large ship in which people travel long distances, especially on a holiday

How Do We Travel?

We choose different vehicles depending on how far we need to travel, the time we have and the cost of travel. Short distances can be covered using bicycles, scooters, motorcycles, buses and cars. We travel to our schools by the school bus and go to a nearby market by a rickshaw, bicycle or scooter. Longer distances are covered using cars, trains, trams, metro rails, buses, trucks, aeroplanes and ships. Train travel has been the most popular form of long distance travel in India. Our grandparents travelled mostly by trains for vacations or to meet family members in far off cities. Recently, air travel has become an easy way of travelling from one city to another. Over the years, many **airline companies** have started flying to many cities within India. This has made long distance travel by air easier and more comfortable. Rockets are required to travel to outer space, like to go to the moon or the planet Mars.

Think through

What kind of vehicles do you think would have been invented if there was no wheel?

Special Vehicles

There are many vehicles that are used for specific purposes. These are called **special vehicles**.

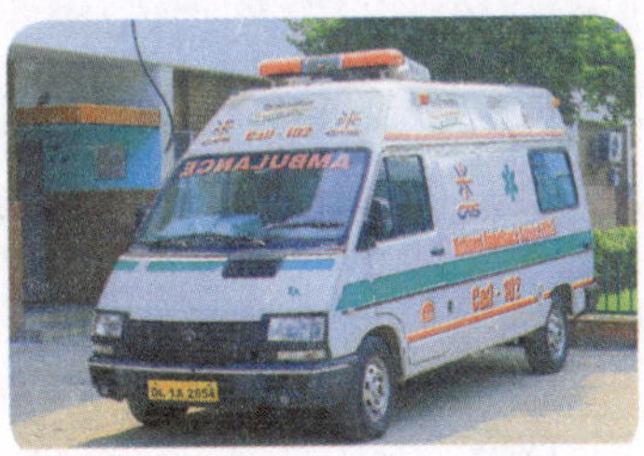

An **ambulance** carries sick and injured people to the hospitals.

A **fire engine** is used for putting out fires.

A **police jeep** carries police officers to help people.

A **mail van** carries letters and parcels from the post office to different parts of the city.

An **ice cream cart** keeps the ice cream frozen.

Vegetable carts are used by vendors to sell vegetables and fruits.

airline companies: companies that manage a particular airline

In the olden days, people walked as much as possible or would cycle to nearby places. Therefore, there were less traffic jams and less air pollution. Nowadays, there are too many vehicles on the roads, which causes frequent traffic jams. This increases the air pollution. We must be careful about using a particular means of transport. We should walk as much as possible and try not to use a vehicle for short distances.

Wrap up

* The first means of travelling from one place to another was by walking, running or swimming.
* The wheel is one of the most important inventions made by human beings.
* Modern-day transport is of three kinds—land, water and air.
* Growing number of vehicles on the road causes air pollution.

Brush up

A Write T for true and F for false.

1. A mail van carries sick people to the hospital. ☐
2. Trains are the fastest way of travelling. ☐
3. The first means of transport was the bullock cart. ☐
4. Trains, trams and metro move on a special metal track. ☐
5. We should try and walk as much as possible. ☐

B Cross (×) the odd one out.

1.	rickshaw	☐	metro	☐	airplane	☐	car	☐
2.	ferry	☐	airplane	☐	ship	☐	boat	☐
3.	fire engine	☐	police van	☐	ice cream cart	☐	truck	☐
4.	car	☐	bus	☐	scooter	☐	bullock cart	☐
5.	glider	☐	airplane	☐	helicopter	☐	bus	☐

C Fill in the blanks.

1. .... and .... are used to carry goods and people on water.
2. A .... carries sick and injured people to the hospital.
3. A .... is a person who checks our tickets on board a train.
4. .... is a special vehicle used to put out fires.
5. A .... is a ship that moves under water.

D Answer these questions.

1. Why do we travel?
2. How did the early humans travel before the wheel was invented?
3. Name the people who work on the railway stations and on the trains. What does each one do?
4. Name some special vehicles. Write what they are used for.
5. What are the reasons for choosing a particular vehicle?

Learn the ropes

Machines are made to make our lives easier and convenient. However, they are also being misused. Write three ways in which machines damage our environment.

Put your heads together

Why is it better to go to school in a bus than in your own car every day? In groups, conduct a class survey with ten classmates. Find out how they come to school. Tick (✓) the right column according to your classmates' answers.

Cross connect

Find out the names of three cities in the world where people use these modes of transport:

Bicycles Cycle rickshaw Trams Boats

17 Means of Communication

Get the ball rolling

What is happening in these pictures. Have you ever tried talking to people without speaking? Have you seen anyone do it?

The Story of Communication

The exchange of information between two or more people is called **communication**. Early humans used sounds, hand **gestures** and signs to communicate with each other. They would draw on the walls of caves to **convey** their messages until they learnt to speak a language.

Ancient paintings on walls of caves

Communication through drawn symbols started thousands of years ago. These symbols were drawn on animal skin or palm leaves and represented different sounds. Human beings began writing with the invention of paper and the letters of the alphabet. In 1443, the invention of the **printing press** made it possible to print many books at the same time.

gestures: a movement of a part of body, especially a hand or head; **convey**: to send from one place to another; **printing press**: a device used for printing newspapers, magazines and books

Means of Communication

People share information by communicating. They communicate using different ways called the **means of communication**. All ways of communicating involve sending and receiving messages. The means of communication are of two types—personal communication and mass communication.

> **Clued in**
>
> Pigeons were used for sending letters that were tied to their feet. Once the bird reached the destination, the letter was removed and the pigeon was sent back with a reply.

Personal Communication

Communicating with one person at a time is called **personal communication**. It takes place between two people, that is, the sender and the receiver. Letters, telephones, mobile phones, fax, email and telegraph are some means of personal communication.

Postal services

Postal services are one of the oldest methods of communication. In India, all cities, towns and most of the villages have post offices. Postcards, inland letters, stamps and stamped envelopes are bought from post offices. They can be sent to any place in India. **Aerogrammes** are used to send letters to people staying in another country.

Postcard

Stamped envelope

Aerogramme

Letters are delivered by means of road, air or water transport such as trains, aeroplanes and ships. Money can be sent from a post office through **money orders**. Gifts are sent as **parcels** to relatives and friends. Letters often take time to reach their destinations. **Speed posts** are used to send a letter to the **destination** in less time. However, they are expensive. A **registered post** is used to send important documents. We can also send letters and parcels through **courier services**. They are faster than normal posts.

Post office

parcels: a thing wrapped in paper to be sent to someone; **destination**: a place to where someone or something is being sent

The journey of a letter

Sara lives in Delhi. She is writing a letter to her friend, Raghu, who lives in Chennai. Let us learn how we post a letter.

Before we post a letter, it should be sealed in a stamped envelope.

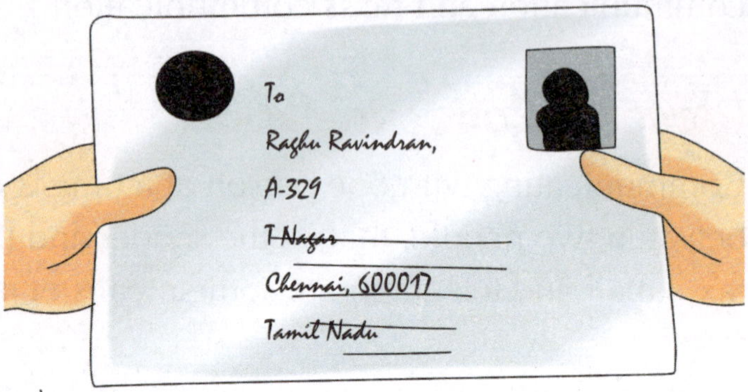

The name of the person to whom we are sending the letter, the address and the **Postal Index Number (PIN)** should be clearly written on the envelope.

The envelope with the letter is then dropped in a nearby **letterbox**. Remember the sender's address should also be written on the envelope.

A **postman** collects all the letters dropped inside the letterbox and takes them to the post office.

Post office seals are stamped on the letters. They are sorted and kept in different boxes according to the destination states and cities.

The letters are then packed in different mailbags and sent to different states and places by road, trains and aeroplanes.

At the post office, letters are stamped and sorted by their areas and addresses.

The letter is delivered to Raghu by the postman on duty for the area.

Communication through telephones

Telephones are the fastest means of communication. We just need to dial the person's phone number to call them. Telephone networks help us to talk to people living in any part of the world. Telephones with wires have been replaced by wireless or cordless telephones. People who do not have telephones, use public call offices or PCOs to make calls by paying a small amount of money.

Cordless telephone

Telephone

Dialling

Calling people living in other states requires a STD code. STD stands for **Subscriber Trunk Dialling**. It is dialled along with the phone number of a person. Therefore, if you are calling a person in Delhi from Pune, you should first dial 011 and then the person's phone number. These codes link people within the country. Calling people outside the country requires an ISD code. It is also dialled along with the phone number. ISD stands for **International Subscriber Dialling**. These codes link people of different countries.

Mobile phones are easy to carry phones that can be used for calling people from anywhere. They are also used to send text messages through **short messaging service** (SMS). **Smartphones** are phones that function with the help of Internet. They work like minicomputers.

Mobile phone

Fax

A fax is used to send an exact copy of a printed or a handwritten document through telephone lines. It can be sent only to a person who has a fax machine.

Fax machine

Communication through computers

Computers are one of the most important modes of communication. One can use an **electronic mail** or **email** for sending videos, pictures, letters and books to anyone and anywhere. The Internet helps us send emails, pictures and videos from one computer to another. People use the Internet to see and talk to each other through video calling. It is important that both the sender and the receiver have Internet connection on their computers.

Computer

Mass Communication

Communicating or sending messages to many people at the same time is known as **mass communication**. Newspapers, magazines, radio, television, Internet, cinema and advertisements are modes of mass communication. They are also known as **mass media**.

Think through

Name the newspapers your parents or grandparents read.

Newspapers and magazines: We read newspapers and magazines to gain knowledge about different events occurring around the world. They are printed sheets of paper, which are published in different languages to make them available to many people.

Radio: It is an instrument which provides information, songs and other programmes through sound, which people can listen to.

Radio

Television: It is one of the most popular means of mass communication. It is an **audio-visual** medium through which news, sports, entertainment, films and other recorded programmes can be viewed.

Film or cinema: It is another audio-visual means of mass communication. Cinema is a source of entertainment for people. It can also be used for educating people.

Television

Computers: Computers are machines that help us get important information such as weather and news reports from all over the world with the help of the Internet. We also send emails from computers. Many computer programmes allow us to make video calls to people across the world.

Internet: It is one of the fastest means of communication. The Internet provides us information from anywhere in the world. It is a vast source of knowledge and information. Shopping and banking can also be done with the help of the Internet.

E-readers and tablets: These are gadgets used for reading books, listening to music, watching films and doing most of the work that we can do on a computer.

Tablet

Give it a shot

Find out the names of some popular newspapers and magazines of India. Write the languages in which they are printed. Cut some interesting news snippets from them and paste them in your notebook.

Newspaper/Magazine	Language

audio-visual: something that you can hear as well as see

Communicating Without Speaking

Sign language

When you were a baby, you could not talk. However, you could still communicate with the adults around you. There are many people who communicate their feelings without speaking. People who cannot talk and hear communicate using signs or hand movements, which is known as the **sign language**. It consists of 26 hand symbols.

Dancers communicate through gestures

Some people can speak and yet they communicate without speaking. They do it through facial expressions, gestures and postures of their bodies. For instance, dancers and theatre artists communicate through movements. Gestures used by dancers are called *mudras*. Their facial expressions are called *bhavas*.

All living things can communicate with each other in different ways. To communicate with each other, it is important to understand each other's language. Communication is a way of expressing our thoughts.

Give it a shot

Let's Play Pictionary!

Work in two groups—Group A and Group B. Ask your teacher to select five words for each group. Students from Group A should draw pictures on the board related to the word given. Group B should guess the word. Repeat the exercise and ask the students of Group B to draw the pictures.

Wrap up

* The exchange of information between two or more people is called communication.
* The two types of communication are personal communication and mass communication.
* Postal communication is one of the oldest methods of communication.
* Telephones are the fastest means of communication.
* Mobiles phones are easy to use as they can be carried anywhere. They are also used to send messages instantly.
* The Internet helps people communicate with others through computers, tablets and mobiles phones.

- Newspaper, magazine, radio and television help us communicate with many people at once. They are also known as mass media.
- People who cannot speak or listen use sign language to communicate.

Brush up

A Fill in the blanks with the correct answers.

1. .... (Radio/Television) is an audio-visual means of communication.
2. .... (Fax machines/Computers) are used with help of an Internet connection.
3. .... (Letters/Emails) are used to send messages to many people at the same time.
4. There are .... (26/28) hand symbols in the sign language.
5. .... (Emails/Money orders) are used to send money.

B Match the following.

1.	ISD	a.	Postal communication
2.	Radio	b.	Messages
3.	Email	c.	Telephone
4.	Postcards	d.	Audio
5.	Mobile phone	e.	Internet

C Fill in the blanks.

1. People who are unable talk and hear use signs or hand movements are known as ....
2. .... is something that you can hear as well as see.
3. .... phones can be carried anywhere.
4. Communicating with one person at a time is known as .... communication.
5. The .... helps us to send out emails, pictures and videos from one computer to another.

D Answer these questions.

1. What is communication?
2. How did early humans communicate with each other?

3. What is a fax machine?
4. What are the two types of communication? Explain any three means of mass communication.
5. What is an email?
6. How do people communicate without speaking?
7. How is the Internet useful to us in communicating with others?
8. How is the television different from radio?

Learn the ropes

Write a letter to your friend explaining your recent visit to a hill station. You will need an inland letter, a postcard and an envelope. Post the letter to your friend from the post office.

Put your heads together

1. Work in pairs. Which means of communication do you prefer and why? Present your reasons on a chart paper. You can also draw or cut out pictures and paste them on the chart.
2. Let's play dumb charades. Use body movements and gestures to describe a word. Ask your classmates to try to guess the word.

Cross connect

Collect ten postage stamps used in India. Paste them in your notebook and describe them. Try collecting some stamps from other countries. You can also make an album using the stamps.

18 Pottery

Get the ball rolling

What kinds of pots do we see around us? Have you seen anyone selling ceramic and earthen pots nearby? Have you ever seen potters working? What do you know about pottery?

Vessels made of clay have been used by people for thousands of years to store food items or water. A type of soil called **clay** mixed with water is used to make such vessels. Early pottery was made by hand to shape the clay. A hole was first made into a ball of clay and then, strips of clay were used to make handles for the vessel. However, these vessels broke very easily and could not store water. Later, people started baking the clay in fire, which made the vessels strong enough to hold water.

Clay vessels

clay: a stiff, sticky fine-grained earth that is moulded when wet, and is dried and baked to make bricks, pottery, and ceramics

Pottery

Pottery

Pottery is one of the oldest forms of art. Objects that are made of wet clay are known as **pottery**. Clay is a soft soil which becomes sticky when mixed with water. It can be moulded into different shapes and then baked in a special oven to make it strong. Pots, jars, dishes, bowls and diyas are some of the examples.

The first step in pottery is to choose the right kind of clay. Some potters add sand, chalk or **husk** to the clay to make it better. Water is added to the clay and **kneaded** to form a **lump**. The clay is then shaped into pots, dishes and bowls. The objects are further baked and decorated.

Shaping Clay

There are various methods of shaping clay. We will learn about two methods—**hand building method** and **wheel method**.

Think through

Why does water kept in a clay pot stay cool?

Hand building method

In this method, people use their hands to press and shape the clay. There are **four** ways to do this. In **pinching** pots are made from a single lump of clay. These pots are made by pinching the clay into the desired shape; no other tools are necessary.

In the **coil method**, the clay is rolled into the shape of a worm or snake and then rolled up into a coil to get the desired size and shape.

In the **slab method** the clay is made flat by using a rolling pin and cut into **slabs**. These slabs are joined to make vessels or containers. The **press mould method** is a method in which clay is forced into a mould to give a shape.

Mould method

Pinching

Slab method

husk: the dry outer covering of some fruits or seeds; **knead**: to work dough or clay into a uniform mixture by pressing, folding and stretching; **lump**: a lump of something is a solid piece of it

The wheel method

The **invention** of the potter's wheel made pottery much simpler. The potter's wheel is a round, flat, wooden or metal surface that spins with the help of a stick. The potter places a round moist ball of clay onto the potter's wheel. A little water is used to smoothen the clay and to hold it in place. The potter then spins the wheel with a stick, or by pressing it with feet. **Motorized** wheels are also used. While the wheel spins, the potter gives shape to the clay with hands and fingers. Once the clay is shaped into the pot, it is removed from the wheel by placing a thread or a knife at the base of the pot. It is kept aside to dry and then finally baked in a special oven known as **kiln**. This makes the pot hard and strong. The pots or vessels are then painted or **glazed** to make it smooth, shiny and **waterproof**.

Potter spinning the wheel with a stick

Removing a pot with knife

Motorized potter's wheel

Pottery in Our Lives

Pottery, in olden days, was used to store water and grains, to cook, and to eat and drink from. People store water in a clay pot in summers as it keeps it cool. Tea is served in clay cups known as *kulhars* in railway stations. Some dishes like kulfi and kheer are made in earthen pots as that gives them a distinct taste. Plants are also grown in clay pots.

Clued in

Pottery is a very important source to learn about the lives of early humans.

Different types of pots are made around the country. Black clay pottery is from Nizamabad in Uttar Pradesh, while Khurja in Uttar Pradesh and Jaipur in Rajasthan are famous for Blue Pottery.

Black clay pottery

Blue pottery

Give it a shot

Make a list of things made of clay. Use the coil method and make different objects.

motorized: specially fitted with an engine or motor; **kiln**: a furnace or oven for burning, baking or drying; **glazed**: cover with a smooth, shiny coating or finish; **waterproof**: a coating that keeps out water

Decorating Pottery

Slip clay decoration

Pottery can be decorated in the wet stage or leathery stage with slip clay. Slip clay is a liquid or semi-liquid mixture of clay. It is used to make designs that create a raised surface. Sometimes, the slip clay used for decorating might be of different colour than the underlying clay body.

Texturing

This is another type of slip decoration method. Slip clay is poured and then textures such as leaves, laces and combs are created using brushes. Once the piece is dried, it is put in fire or baked.

Engraving or etching

Engraving or etching process starts at the leather-hard stage. The tools used to do this are pencil, pin or any sharp and pointed tool. Then it is baked.

With paints

These are ways in which pottery – which is not used for eating or drinking purposes – is decorated by painting it. Painting is used for decorating pots, diyas, wall hangings and terracotta ornaments.

The paintings are done using acrylic paints. First, the base colour is painted and then a design is made on the pottery. Designs can be motifs of flowers, block prints or traditional paintings such as Pattachitra, Madhubani and Warli. To give the acrylic paint a shine, it is painted with varnish.

Wrap up

* Objects made of wet clay are known as pottery.
* The early pottery was made by just pushing a hole into a ball of clay.
* In olden days, people used their hands to give shape to clay for making different objects.
* In olden days, pottery was used as container to store water and grains, also to cook, and to eat and drink from.
* They learnt that baking clay pots in fire makes them stronger.
* A step-by-step process is used in pottery, where clay is kneaded, shaped, baked and decorated.
* There are different methods to shape the clay by hand building method and wheel method.
* In many houses, people use different clay pots for different purposes.

Brush up

A Fill in the blanks with the correct answers.

1. Clay is a soft soil which becomes .... when mixed with water.
   a. smooth   b. sticky   c. silky
2. Black clay pottery is from .... in Uttar Pradesh.
   a. Ghaziabad   b. Allahabad   c. Nizamabad
3. Khurja in Uttar Pradesh and Jaipur in Rajasthan are famous for .... Pottery.
   a. Blue   b. Black   c. Brown
4. Pottery can be decorated in the wet stage with .... clay.
   a. drip   b. flat   c. slip
5. A tool used for etching is ....
   a. brush   b. rolling pin   c. pencil

B Arrange the step-by-step process of pot making in the correct sequence.

1. Water is added to clay, kneaded with hands and then made into a lump. ☐
2. The clay is shaped into pots, dishes and bowls. ☐
3. The right kind of clay is chosen. ☐
4. The objects are decorated. ☐
5. The objects are baked. ☐

C Write T for true and F for false.

1. Assam is known for Blue Pottery.
2. Potter's wheel helps to make clay objects faster.
3. Sometimes clay is forced into a mould to give it a shape.
4. Pottery is one of the modern arts of the world.

D Answer these questions.

1. What is pottery?
2. What are the different methods of shaping clay?
3. What is a potter's wheel?
4. Explain the wheel method of shaping clay.
5. Write the uses of pottery in our lives.
6. Explain these terms:
   a. kiln b. pottery c. pinching
7. Describe two methods of pottery decoration.

Learn the ropes

'Potters are facing problems due to change in lifestyle.' Discuss this issue in class. How can we help them?

Put your heads together

Visit a nearby potter and collect clay scraps that are left over while trimming. Bring these scraps to school. Work in groups and dump all the clay scraps in a bucket of water, enough to cover the clay. Use the softened clay to make any decorative item of your choice. You can use them to decorate your classroom.

Cross connect

Visit a potter and see how he or she works with the potter's wheel. Write a short paragraph about what you saw.

19 From Fibre to Fabric

Get the ball rolling

Have you seen these dresses before? Do you know how they are made?

We wear clothes to protect ourselves from the changing weather and to look good. Early humans used to wear leaves, barks of trees, fur and animal skin to protect themselves from the weather. This was before humans learnt how to stich and make cloth. Gradually, humans learnt how to grow **natural fibres** like cotton, silk, jute and wool. Over the years they learnt **spinning** these **fibre**s into thread and then weaving the threads to make it into **fabric** or cloth.

> **Clued in**
>
> The earliest cotton in the world was spun and worn in India. This trend was so popular that even Roman emperors would buy and wear cotton from India.

Weaving

Weaving is the process of making cloth or fabric from thread or fibre. Thread can be made from natural fibres such as cotton, silk, wool or jute or from **artificial** fibres like **nylon** and

spinning: make thread from cotton or wool by twisting them; **fibre**: material, such as, wool and cotton; **artificial:** made or produced by human beings

polyester. Weaving is done on machines called **looms** that can be worked by hand or on electricity. The looms worked by hand are called **handlooms** and those that run on electricity are called **power looms**. Two lengths of thread are woven into each other to weave fibre into fabric. Saree, pants, shirts, school uniform, salwar kameez, lungi and dhotis are all made from cloth that is woven.

Power loom

Handloom

Knitting

Besides weaving, knitting is another process to make cloth. Knitting is mostly done with wool to make sweaters, caps, mufflers, gloves and socks. You might have seen your grandmother knitting with **knitting needles** at home. Knitting, like weaving, can be done by hand as well as by knitting machines. T-shirts, track pants, swimwear and underclothes are some clothes that are made from fabric knitted on machines.

Knitting

Colour My Cloth

Many times the threads of the cotton, silk or woollen fibre are coloured before they are woven or knitted to make cloth. Sometimes the cloth is made first and then coloured. This process of colouring the cloth to get the colour we like is called **dyeing**. You must have seen your mother getting her dupatta dyed in the market. Have you ever observed the dyeing process?

Cloth dye

Cloth dyeing

The dyer mixes several colours and makes a solution in water to get the exact colour of your liking. The cloth is then put in that coloured solution and heated for some time. The cloth takes the colour of the solution. Finally, the cloth is taken out of the solution. The excess water is squeezed out and then the cloth is dried. The dyer in the market can dye small lengths of cloth. When a lot of fabric needs to be dyed, it is done in factories. We buy this coloured or dyed cloth from the market

> **Think through**
>
> Why should we wear woollen clothes in winters and cotton clothes in summers?

and get it stitched to our needs. Dyes that are made from chemicals are called **chemical dyes**. Dyes that are made from natural products such as fruits, vegetables, flowers and other parts of a plant are called **vegetable dyes**.

Designs and Patterns

In shops, we get cloth that is not only dyed in different colours, but also have different designs and patterns to make it look beautiful and attractive. Designs and patterns are made in several ways.

Tie and dye is a traditional and popular method used widely in Rajasthan and Gujarat. The cloth is tied in different ways and then dyed to get attractive patterns.

Tie and dye

In **block printing**, beautiful designs **carved** on wooden blocks are dipped in colours and then pressed on the cloth in interesting patterns.

Block printing

The concept of block printing is also used with vegetables. A vegetable like potato or ladies' finger is cut and dipped in paint and used to make attractive designs on cloth. This process is called **vegetable printing**.

Vegetable printing

Screen printing designs are made on a screen and then copied on the cloth using colours.

Screen printing

carved: a design made in a wooden piece by taking out portions of the wood

Give it a shot

Get a white handkerchief that you no longer use and one ladies' finger from home. In class, mix some colours to create new colour shades. Cut the ladies' finger and dip it in the colour, and then press it on the handkerchief to make patterns. Display the beautiful handkerchiefs in class.

Batik designs are made by dyeing a cloth that has wax on it. The wax is removed to show the beautiful and **intricate** designs on the cloth. Batik is very popular in West Bengal.

Batik

Beautiful designs with shapes and flowers are **embroidered** on a cloth. Embroidery can be done by hand or by machines.

Embroidery

Unstitched Clothes

Clothes can be stitched or unstitched. We mostly wear stitched clothes like shirt, pant, skirt and top, kurta and pyjama, and salwar kameez, which are cut and stitched out of a piece of cloth. A cloth that is not cut and stitched, but worn by wrapping it around the body is called an unstitched cloth.

Different types of sarees

The traditional Indian dress for women is the **saree**. A saree is a six yards long unstitched piece of cloth. But the saree too has great variety and is worn in different styles across the country. The length of the saree is also different in the different states.

Different types of dhotis

intricate: detailed and complex; **embroidered**: patterns made on clothes with different coloured threads

Like women, men too wear the unstitched fabric in the form of a **lungi** or **dhoti**. The lungi is also worn in different ways in different regions of India.

Dupattas

A **dupatta** is another type of unstitched cloth, however, it is much shorter in length than a saree. A dupatta is called by different names like *chunni*, *odhni* and *chunari*, in different parts of the country. The dupatta is also worn in different ways in the different states of India.

Different types of turbans

The **turban** or the **pagdi** is a long, unstitched piece of cloth wrapped on the heads of men. It is worn differently in different states of India. It is worn to cover the head.

Shawls

A **shawl** is an unstitched cloth made of wool. It is worn by both men and women in the winter to keep warm. The most famous shawls are the **Pashmina** shawls of Kashmir. They are the made of fine woollen cloth with beautiful embroidery.

A lot of hard work by many different people goes into making the clothes we wear. We must make sure that we wear clean and washed clothes every day. This keeps us healthy, makes us look good and gives us confidence. In a country like India, where it is hot most of the year, we wear clothes made from cotton. Cotton is a natural fibre that is easy on our skin, it does not irritate the skin or cause rashes during the hot summer months. For people who work in the kitchen, it is important to wear cotton clothes and not clothes made of nylon or polyester.

We wear clothes according to the climate of the place we live in and culture and customs of the region we come from. The clothes we wear differ from region to region in our country. Latest fashion in colours, designs and styles also determines what we wear at a particular time. Special occasions like marriages and other parties are times when people dress up in their best. All over India, you will mostly see men wearing pants or jeans and shirts, and women wearing sarees, salwar kameez or jeans and shirt. However, the different states of our country also have their own traditional dresses.

Pashmina: very fine Kashmiri wool

Types of Clothes

A pheran

The traditional dresses of Jammu and Kashmir have beautiful embroidery and **delicate** designs. The men and women in this cold mountainous region wear clothes made from wool to keep themselves warm and comfortable. **Pherans** and *poots* are worn by the people in Kashmir. These are two gowns worn one on top of the other. These gowns are long and fall till below the knees and are sometimes worn with a salwar.

The Punjabi suit or the salwar suit is the traditional dress of women in Punjab. This comprises of the kameez, which is the long shirt worn with a salwar. They are worn with a matching or contrasting dupatta. Men wear a long kurta over a lungi or *tehmat*.

Punjabi clothes

A woman wearing a Maharashtrian saree

A Maharashtrian style pagri

The traditional clothes of Maharashtra are colourful. Men usually wear a **dhoti** or, as it is sometimes called, a *dhotar* and a *pheta* which is a headdress, a *pagri* or a *topi* usually made of cotton. A kurta or a shirt is worn over the dhoti. Sometimes Maharashtrian men wear a waistcoat called *bundi*, which is a sleeveless jacket worn over a shirt or *kurta*. Women wear sarees that are nine yards long and are tucked in the middle, making them look like dhotis. This type of saree is called a *lugda* or *nauvari*. A *choli* or blouse is worn with the saree. These sarees are made from cotton or silk.

A man wearing a mundu and a shirt

Traditionally, men and women in Kerala wear white clothes. Both men and women wear a lungi called *mundu* that is worn around the waist. It has a border called *kara*, which can be of any colour, but it is mostly golden. Men mostly wear the mundu with a shirt. Women wear two mundus called the *mundum-neriyathum*—one worn around the waist falling to the ankles like a skirt, and the other worn on top with a blouse like a saree.

Wrap up

- Every region in India has its own traditional dress.
- Once the fabric or the cloth is ready, it is dyed and then designed with beautiful patterns or embroidery.
- Fabric can be designed in many ways like tie and dye, batik, block and screen printing.
- Clothes are worn according to the climate and the customs and traditions of the region.

Brush up

A Fill in the blanks.

1. .... and .... are worn by people in Kashmir.
2. Threads are woven into fabric by ....
3. An unstitched cloth worn around the waist by men in Kerala is called .... and in Punjab is called ....
4. An unstitched cloth worn to cover the head by men is called ....
5. .... is the process of colouring cloth.

B Write T for true or F for false.

1. The process of knitting is used to make socks. ☐
2. Saree and dupatta are both unstitched clothes. ☐
3. Tie and dye is widely used in Karnataka. ☐
4. Vegetable dyes are obtained from fruits, flowers and other parts of a plant. ☐
5. Printing, embroidery and painting are all ways of making a fabric beautiful. ☐

C Match the following.

1.	Shawl	a.	Mundu
2.	Batik	b.	Gloves
3.	Dupatta	c.	Kashmir
4.	Dhoti	d.	West Bengal
5.	Knitting	e.	*Chunari*

D Answer these questions.

1. List the reasons why we wear different types of clothes.
2. What did the early humans wear and why?
3. What is the difference between weaving and knitting?
4. How is a cloth coloured?
5. What are the different ways in which a cloth can be made to look pretty?

Learn the ropes

As growing children, you could be outgrowing your clothes fast. While it is a good idea to recycle old clothes by giving them to someone you know, it is an equally good idea to make something new from these old clothes. Take your old jeans or pyjamas and cut them into long strips. Ask a tailor to stitch all these pieces together. You can use this patchwork cloth as your table cover.

Put your heads together

Get different pieces of cloth from home. In groups, stick these pieces of cloth on a chart and write if the fibre used is natural or man-made. If it is natural, mention whether it is cotton, silk, jute or wool. If it is man-made, mention whether it is nylon or polyester.

Cross connect

If the length of your school shirt is 20 inches, taking the help of your maths teacher, find out how much cloth will you need to buy to make a shirt for yourself. If the cloth you buy is ₹100 per metre, find out how much money will you need to buy cloth for one shirt.

Crafts of India

India has a rich and a diverse tradition of crafts. Each state and region of India has its own special style and form of crafts.

Metal Work of Bidar

Handicrafts made of metal in the small town of Bidar in Karnataka are also known as **Bidriware**. A mixture of some metals is poured in moulds to get the shape of the item being made, which is then given a black coating. Very thin sheets or wires of pure silver are put in the designs carved in the piece.

Madhubani Painting of Bihar

Madhubani painting originated in Mithila region of Bihar and is also called Mithila painting. In these paintings, different shapes are used to represent traditions and festivals. Twigs, matchsticks and even fingers are used to make these paintings using natural and vegetable colours.

Cane and Bamboo Work of Assam

Furniture, baskets, lamp shades, fans and many other items are woven and made from cane and bamboo in Assam. These products are made without any machines, completely by hand. The products made in Assam are different and have their own unique style and designs. Fishing equipment used by the fishermen are also made from bamboo.

Marble Inlay Art of Uttar Pradesh

This beautiful art work done on marble is also called *Parchinkari*. This work can be found in the Taj Mahal. Shapes, flowers and birds are first engraved on the marble piece. These are then filed with coloured marble, glass pieces or gem stones. This is delicate hand work and takes a lot of hard work and time.

Kantha Work of Bengal

West Bengal has a rich tradition of weaving and embroidery. Their sarees have bright colours from the traditional handloom embroidery technique called **kantha**. This is a simple running stitch used to create beautiful designs full of flowers, birds, animals and shapes. The kantha stitch gives a wavy effect to the fabric.

Block Printing of Rajasthan

Wooden blocks which have beautiful designs **carved** on them are used in block printing. These wooden blocks are dipped in paint or colours and then pressed on the cloth in interesting patterns. The colours that are used in this could be either chemical or vegetable colours. The concept of block printing is also used with vegetables. Instead of a wooden block, a vegetable like ladies' finger is cut and dipped in paint, and used to make attractive designs on cloth. This process is called **vegetable printing**.

Stay Safe

It is important to follow these steps to stay safe during the pandemic.

Help the doctor find her way to the cure.

Suggested Assessment 1

Maximum Marks: 30

A Match the following. 2.5

1.	From parents to children	a.	Child labour
2.	Dyeing	b.	Insects
3.	Children employed for money	c.	Indoor games
4.	Ladybirds	d.	Indigo
5.	Playing on a tablet	e.	Hereditary features

B Fill in the blanks with the correct answers. 2.5

1. Carbohydrates and fats are .... food.
   a. energy-giving b. body-building food c. protective food
2. .... will use the Braille.
   a. A deaf person b. An old person c. A blind person
3. Lizards have a long sticky ....
   a. Tail b. Tongue c. Limb
4. .... live in old age homes.
   a. Orphans b. Young people c. Old people
5. A .... is a small to medium-sized hard, woody plant.
   a. tree b. shrub c. herb

C Write T for true and F for false. 2.5

1. A family tree starts with the first generation. ☐
2. Meat and eggs are sent to the markets from dairy farms. ☐
3. Games played in the old days involved team work. ☐
4. The green stem which contains chlorophyll prepares water. ☐
5. Children who work get paid more than adults. ☐

D Fill in the blanks. 5

1. Shedding of leaves helps plants to .... water.
2. Families in which children stay with either the mother or the father are called .... families.
3. The work that people do to earn their living is their ....

4. Earthworms cannot fly, they .... and crawl.
5. Animals that are in danger of becoming extinct are known as ....

E Unscramble the following words. 2.5

1. PHYCOLOLYRL ....
2. NABODEM ....
3. TIMANIV ....
4. ATLON ....
5. ATHGRAFERND ....

F Answer these questions. 12

1. Write two ways in which we can help old people.
2. What is a poultry farm?
3. How is a sportsperson different from a professional player?
4. What are the ways in which you can help with house work?
5. Who camouflages and why?
6. Why are leaves known as food factories?

G Draw and label the parts of a leaf. 3

Suggested Assessment 2

Maximum Marks: 30

A Match the following. 2.5

1.	Brick and cement	a.	Tube well
2.	26 hand symbols	b.	Steaming
3.	Mundu	c.	Double-storeyed houses
4.	Groundwater	d.	Sign language
5.	Pressure cooker	e.	Kerala

B Fill in the blanks with the correct answers. 2.5

1. Food cooked rapidly over a high heat while stirring fast is called ....
   a. stir-frying   b. deep frying   c. shallow frying
2. Pheran is worn in ....
   a. West Bengal   b. Jammu and Kashmir   c. Assam
3. .... is a means of mass communication.
   a. Letter   b. Radio   c. Fax
4. Nowadays maps have been replaced by ....
   a. compass   b. books   c. GPS
5. .... carries letters and parcels from the post office.
   a. Mail van   b. Ambulance   c. Fire engine

C Write T for true and F for false. 2.5

1. Water in liquid form has a fixed shape and size. ☐
2. Women wear a turban to cover their heads. ☐
3. When food is cooked in less oil, it is called shallow frying. ☐
4. A building that has many apartments in it is called a double-storeyed house. ☐
5. Texturing is a type of slip decoration method. ☐

D Fill in the blanks. 2.5

1. A .... house can be destroyed by heavy rain and strong winds.
2. To communicate with each other we need to understand each other's ....
3. A .... is used to understand the symbols on a map.

4. .... is one of the very first ways of travelling.

5. Domestic animals depend on human beings for .... , ... and water.

E Unscramble the following words. 2.5

1. SENTUIL ....
2. ROPTEYT ....
3. ADRUM ....
4. ACNEO ....
5. PETS ....

F Complete the crossword puzzle with the help of the given clues. 5

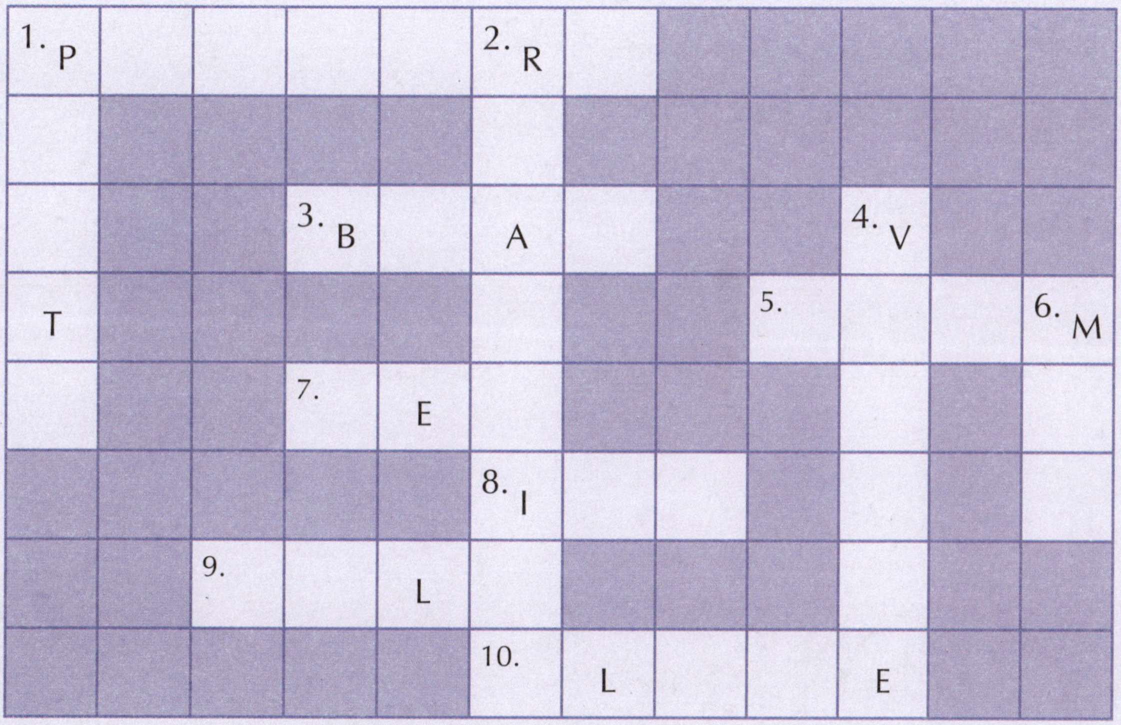

Across

1. Objects made of wet clay
3. Communicating through facial expressions
5. Weaving is done on these machines
7. Doctor who treats animals
8. It is the solid form of water
9. A furnace for baking clay
10. A model of the Earth

Down

1. Unwanted animals in our houses
2. When food is roasted by cooking over an open fire
4. It is the space enclosed in a container
6. It is a drawing of city or country on a flat surface like paper

G Name them. 2.5

1. Water that is clean and fit for drinking is ....
2. Boats that are modified to be used as a house ....
3. These are used by people to travel ....
4. A thing that is used to send letters to people staying in another country ....
5. Machines used to weave fabric ....

H Answer these questions. 5

1. How is a cloth dyed?
2. Why are some animals that enter our house called harmful animals?
3. Why are symbols used in a plan?
4. What is baking?
5. How does an igloo keep people warm?
6. What is hand building method in pottery?

I Draw and label the water cycle. 5